The Be-Attitudes of Chaplaincy

Jo Jensen

Whatif Publishing

THE BE-ATTITUDES OF CHAPLAINCY

First Edition, 2015

Formatted by Robin Thomas
Cover Design by Linda Boulanger
Edited by Kirsten T. Talbot

I have tried to recreate events, locales, and conversations from my memories and journal entries of them. In order to maintain their anonymity, in some instances I have changed the names of individuals and places, and I may have changed some identifying characteristics and details such as physical properties, occupations, and places of residence. In other instances I have obtained permission to use exact names.

Library of Congress Control Number: 2015902437
ISBN: 978-0692385371

Whatif Publishing
Austin

PRINTED IN THE UNITED STATES OF AMERICA

To my treasured friend Judy Eliott. Her friendship, insight, humor, and unwavering faith in God infused me with the inspiration to hear the call to chaplaincy and instilled in me the determination to pursue that call despite my perceived obstacles. I am forever grateful for the countless ways Judy's endearing and enduring friendship lives on, enriching my life in unimaginable ways.

To my father, Larry Jensen. His unconditional love and steadfast encouragement were gifts in my youth and sustained me in later years. My father taught me to believe in myself, respect others, engage humor, be responsible, and never, ever give up. It is my prayer that this body of work honors his life, memory, and uncompromising belief in a daughter whose love for him extends beyond the grave.

Acknowledgements

This book bears the imprint of many people who encouraged me from inception to completion. It is with great pleasure that I offer these words of appreciation to many whose relationships and interactions made this document possible.

I am most grateful to Dr. Ann-Marie Neale. Although choosing Dr. Neale as my Doctoral Project Consultant initially appeared to be random, I soon realized the decision had divine origins. It is difficult to overstate my gratitude for the early inspiration, tireless dedication to perfection, and unceasing source of encouragement Dr. Neale provided throughout the project. Dr. Neale's creative genius, keen eye, and charming sense of humor inspired me to be tenacious in achieving my goal. I am immensely thankful for her candid suggestions, unwavering dedication, shared stories, and generous laughter.

I wish to thank Rev. Jenny Lannom, who did much more than supervise me through a year of Clinical Pastoral Education (CPE). Jenny's uncanny knack for focusing on my skills and strengths permitted my growing edges to become smoother in the process. I am especially grateful for Jenny's extraordinary wisdom, insight, and blossoming friendship in the years since CPE. Words cannot fully express my appreciation to Jenny for her gracious Foreword to this book.

I offer special words of thanks to the late Dr. Virginia Unverzagt and to Dr. Richard Collins of St. Mary-of-the-Woods College, who stimulated my writing skills and enthusiastically encouraged me to pursue a Doctor of Ministry degree.

I am indebted and immeasurably grateful to the wise women in my life whose longstanding friendships and support have nurtured my spirit in ways that defy description. Thank you to the late Ellie Buczek, Jacqui Pequignot, Pam Steinke, Louise Westlake, and Kathy Wilson for your encouragement and support.

To my writing mentor, Teresa Burrell, I offer my heartfelt appreciation for years of friendship laden with uproarious laughter, unquestioning support in times of trouble, and the ways and means to publishing that prevented months—perhaps years—of personal pain and research. You have been a great gift introduced to me by my eldest brother!

Thank you to the myriad medical team members in New Mexico, Florida, and Texas, whose unique talents, support, referrals, and trust propelled me to take an inclusive, active role in the interdisciplinary patient-centered care at their facilities.

Thank you from the bottom of my heart to the countless patients and families who permitted me to sit with them in their suffering and walk alongside them in times of joy. I am sincerely honored and genuinely humbled to have been a vessel into which they birthed the sacred stories of their lives.

And finally, but most significantly, to my husband, Bob, who is a fountain of encouragement and patience. I am more grateful than words can possibly convey for his "glass-half-full" approach to life. He listened patiently as I read segments of this book to him. He offered perspective that was both constructive and supportive. He is my rock!

TABLE OF CONTENTS

Foreword

When Jo asked me to write the Foreword for her Doctor of Ministry (D.Min.) project, I was humbled and a bit apprehensive. I was humbled by Jo's confidence in me, and I didn't want to disappoint her, so I said "yes" immediately. Only after saying "yes" did I have some fears that I would not be able to do her work justice. But saying "yes" bolstered me because I believe what Jo has written is a credit to the profession of chaplaincy. I wanted to affirm her creative work, which incorporates photography, story-telling, and poetry to communicate what professional chaplains offer to people in need of spiritual and emotional support. I believe her writing should eventually be published because it would be an invaluable resource for persons who have an "inkling" that they would like to be a chaplain. I also have a more selfish motive. I would love for it to be available as a curriculum resource in seminaries and CPE centers.

I first met Jo in 2004 when she applied to the CPE program I was supervising. Even at that time, I could tell she was a good writer. Her CPE application captured my attention with its engaging style. She has only gotten better over the last 10 years! I believe that Jo is at heart a story weaver. Her ministry focuses on hearing with clarity the patient's story and engaging their story with such compassion and care that she becomes a part of the fabric of it for a time.

Jo engages people on the edges of life. When people have a health crisis, particularly cancer, they can feel as if the bottom has dropped out of their world and they are standing on a precipice. At such a time, if they are fortunate, a chaplain engages them to offer emotional and spiritual support, offering them space to reflect on the meaning of this intrusive, and at first horrible, interloper in their lives. But if Jo is their chaplain, they will be greatly blessed. I say this because Jo has a special gift of empathy. They will feel heard and understood. They will feel validated as one who is walking a unique path. They will be greatly blessed because Jo is open to what Thomas Merton called, "allowing God to wear our face." It matters not your age or station in life. Jo meets all with an openness, a kindness, and a sense of humor that is blessed by God.

People often share with me, and I imagine with most chaplains, that they cannot imagine doing what I do. They often say things like, "It must be so sad being around death all the time." But chaplains like Jo know the real truth: It is some of the most holy work we are privileged to do because we journey with people who are searching and struggling for meaning and purpose, often at the exigencies of life. When illness strikes, often like a lightning bolt, it leaves us disoriented and often terribly fearful and anxious. It is at times like this that each of us needs a skilled, caring, and sensitive person to listen and let us know that whatever we are feeling and experiencing is just right to feel and experience. When that happens, we look for someone to walk with us so we do not feel so alone. If we are fortunate, we may have family who can sit and listen and not try to cheerlead us into a new perspective. In my experience, however, this is incredibly rare, not because our families are insensitive and do not really love us, but because they love us and are so close to us that the thought of us suffering with illness is too much for them to bear. Most caring families want to take the suffering away. Chaplains are trained to learn how to create a space for suffering, to listen to it and honor it, to even hold it for a time, but then give it back to the patient like the bourgeoning gift that it is. Because, in the end, only the patient can walk this path. In the end, the patient decides whether suffering has meaning or not. With God's help, only the patient can work to make suffering transformational. It is no one else's work...it is not the work of one's friends, or one's family, or one's chaplain. This is the truth that Jo knows and practices.

Jo has always impressed me as a bit of a "funny duck." I say this because she entered CPE from a very lucrative and successful career in computer technology. It requires a person to live in their left-brain most of the time and be a problem solver. Many times, though not all of course, technology is not a "people-oriented" field. But even as a manager in her field, Jo was a people person. The staff she managed loved her. I often wondered how someone of her talent and gifts survived and thrived in that world. But she did. At some point, however, she realized that she had a call to serve people in a different way.

I am aware that the concept of a "call" to ministry is not universally experienced by all faith/spiritual traditions. Rather it seems to be a uniquely Christian concept. So if this is a new concept for you, let me take a moment and try to paint a picture of what it means to be "called."

In Judeo-Christian scriptures, the story of God often gets told through relationships between God and God's people. The story of God "calling" Moses to lead the Hebrews out of slavery was a story of call and response. The story of Hannah offering her son, Samuel, in service to God, and then God calling Samuel into leadership in ancient Israel as a prophet, is another such story. The scriptures are replete with stories of God engaging people to do the work that God wants done. Usually in the story of a call, people hear a "voice." Sometimes the voice is audible, and sometimes it is only heard from within one's heart. And sometimes the call comes through the voice of another, like Jo's friend Judy, whom she speaks about in chapter one. It is not unusual when a person begins to sense a call to ministry that the call begins to be echoed by others around them. In almost all instances, the one who is being called does not immediately recognize the call themselves.

At some point in her life, Jo began to hear a call from God to serve others. Perhaps she began to hear it as she volunteered at her local hospice, where she developed her "Into Your Hands" ministry based on Jesus' cry on the cross, "Into Your hands, I commend my spirit." This ministry consisted of her first blessing the dying patient's hands. Next, she would drape their arms with cloth so that just their hands were showing. Lastly, she would carefully position their hands and take a black and white photo. Her photography was an unusual and unique last gift for families to remember their loved one's hands, hands that had served them throughout their lives cooking, holding, carrying, working, tilling, and loving. The photograph was a visual reminder that their loved one was now in the hands of God. Jo utilized her own camera, and developed the pictures at her own expense. It was in this incredible gesture that Jo's imagination, creativity, and heart for ministry was developing.

As with many stories of call, Jo at first resisted. After all, following one's heart voice is very risky. What if I didn't hear it correctly? How can I give up the security of a job, health insurance, and perhaps a pension to go back to school to study for the ministry? It's crazy, right? Well, perhaps. When we are called, we may resist for a time, but ultimately, we give in because, at some level of consciousness, we sense that staying where we are is not as life-giving as saying "yes" to the Voice. Frederick Buechner put it this way, "The place God calls you to is the place where your deep gladness and the world's deep hunger meet." (Wishful Thinking: A Theological ABC)

Jo talks about many characteristics that professional chaplains need to exhibit and cultivate. She references a love of people, empathy, compassion, and boundaries. One of the characteristics that makes Jo a wonderful professional chaplain is her sense of humor. That may surprise the reader because folks typically do not imagine that chaplains are anything but overly serious and overtly pious people. Good chaplains cultivate a healthy sense of humor. Jo has a "quirky" sense of humor. She has filled my lexicon with a myriad of colloquialisms from West Texas. I, too, grew up in Texas, but on the other side of the state in Houston. I had never heard these sayings before, and when Jo said them, I often would burst out laughing. One of my favorites speaks to someone who looks like they have been through a lot: At the end of CPE, she said, "I feel like a horse that was rode hard and put up wet," a reference to a horse that galloped over a long journey and was not properly wiped down afterward.

A sense of humor is a spiritual resource that helps the professional caregiver avoid burnout and be alert to the subtle surprises of God. Jo speaks about this in her last chapter. A sense of humor is vital and key to self-care of any professional, but particularly for chaplains. It may seem callous to some to imagine laughter in the same paragraph as suffering. I am not talking about the kind of humor stand-up comics use. Professional chaplains do not walk into a patient's room and begin a comedy routine. We do not laugh at the suffering person, but rather walk with the person as the patient identifies some of the ironies of life, and when appropriate, chaplains may offer a sense of perspective or re-framing. Humor is utilized with sensitive timing and usually follows the patient's lead. Jo is a master at it.

I suppose, more than anything, Jo's writing offers us a glimpse into a person who truly loves others and has offered her life to be "with" them in a very real, incarnational way; so that when she parts from them, people feel they have been touched by the presence of the Divine through her care. That is something I cannot teach. It is a gift from God.

Rev. Jenny Lannom, BCC, ACPE Supervisor
Lakewood, Colorado
January 20

Introduction

As I write this, a milestone birthday looms large. In a mere three weeks I will be sixty-five years old. Not only did I not anticipate becoming a "senior citizen," but neither did I expect to be writing a paper as a concluding component for a Doctor of Ministry (D. Min.) degree. As a matter of fact, when I first stepped foot on this academic path, I shared with my father that I was having as much difficulty imagining the work involved in achieving a D.Min. as I was with accepting being sixty-five. My dad, whose support and humor I have always appreciated, promptly retorted, "Well, you're going to be sixty-five anyway. You might as well be sixty-five with a Doctor of Ministry degree."

Dad was eighty-nine at the time, confined to a nursing home due to the cumulative effects to his left side from several small strokes. Yet he possessed the intellect, charm, and wit of a thirty-year-old. My father's death in 2010, prior to Christmas and just before his ninetieth birthday, had a dual impact on me. Initially, overwhelming grief stymied my interest and subsequently all progress toward my academic goals. But then a few weeks later, in one of those just-before-waking dreams, my father, who had been unable to walk for years, invited me to dance with him. I was a child again, standing on his feet as he danced me around the living room floor. Dad looked down at me with his ever-gentle, always encouraging smile and whispered softly, "Remember, you're going to be sixty-five anyway. You might as well be sixty-five with a Doctor of Ministry degree." As he twirled me around, let go of my hands, and faded out of sight, I heard him say, "I am so proud of you! One and one!" The "one and one" comment was a reference to how we ended all our conversations ever since the first time Dad heard Paul Simon's song "Father and Daughter." Part of the chorus contains these words: "*As long as one and one is two/There could never be a father/Who loved his daughter more than I love you.*" That dream and my father's words propelled me out of bed and back in front of the computer with determined energy for the labor necessary to birth the project I had begun.

Now with that project completed and the process of having it published in sight, I reflect on the ways in which many significant endings in my life have also stimulated adventurous beginnings and the similarity of those seedling beginnings to a pregnancy and birthing process.

The tiny kernel of a notion for the project began on a plain piece of easel paper on which I jotted down unedited characteristics, expectations, functions, and experiences of a chaplain in simple words and phrases. Within a few days, notes on the paper looked more organized than I expected, taking the form of a century-old concept called *mind mapping*. In computer terms, it would be called a core dump, where specific areas of memory within the computer are printed for technology engineers to analyze, diagnose, or debug the reason a program unexpectedly halted. More often than not, this snapshot of the computer's memory at a precise moment in time reveals answers to the immediate problem.

As I continued jotting down the words from my own core memory, the embryo of an idea began to take root and grow. Finally, after many months of incubation, conscientious attention, and early morning writing sessions, *The Be-Attitudes of Chaplaincy* was born.

As with any other vocation, those who feel called to chaplaincy possess qualities and personalities too varied to list; however, as I considered what I thought to be the most basic characteristics, nine distinct words surfaced. Each phrase on my easel paper related to or could be summarized by those nine words. Books and articles have been written that elaborate on various important aspects of chaplaincy such as how to perform a spiritual assessment or be a listening presence. They are magnificent contributions to the field. I have listed a number of them in the suggested reading section at the end of this book.

Choosing specific words and converting them to chapters came about through my personal love for and reflection on the "Beatitudes" in Christian scripture and the Eightfold Path of Buddhism. Rather than comparing and contrasting the profound words of Christ and Buddha, I decided to honor the brevity of each by being as succinct as possible in the selection of words to address the ministry of chaplaincy. Perhaps the notion to do so, in some way, also relates to and honors the ability of a chaplain to be a great listener. Rabbi Abraham Heschel once quipped that "God created people because he loves stories." I would add that God calls people to chaplaincy because God's people need to have their stories birthed and heard.

To illustrate the meaning of the *"be-attitude,"* each chapter contains a narrative selected from my experiences as a chaplain. Names and identifying information of the people whose stories are shared have been modified to protect their privacy, unless the parties have given me specific permission to tell their story.

Because I believe giving birth, in all its forms, signifies and honors the never-ending process of creation, I have also chosen to surround the stories with additional modes of expression. Each chapter begins with a photograph taken by me that is underscored by a recognizable quote. A poem that I composed follows each photograph and is accented with a word or words referencing the *be-attitude.* Just before the chapter narrative is another quote from a famous author that leads into each story. Many of the quotations come from a personal anthology and have helped give meaning to events or situations in my own life. Following each narrative is a prayer I composed to illustrate and summarize the chapter. All nine of the prayers contain a *prayer within a prayer* and so can be read twice, first from beginning to end, then just the larger uniquely scripted words. These prayers are recaptured in a composite prayer book, showing each prayer in its entirety followed by its simpler form.

Throughout the book, I have inserted small *butterfly boxes* to emphasize points that were especially significant to me and may also be of interest to the reader. In the creation of these boxes, I considered them to be tiny notes of wisdom gained through the experiences presented in each chapter. The meaning that butterflies have in my life and my use of them throughout *The Be-Attitudes of Chaplaincy* will become apparent after reading the first chapter.

At the conclusion of each chapter, I have written a series of reflective questions for readers to contemplate, journal, or stimulate discussion with others. Since chaplaincy is an inward journey as well as an outward one, readers are invited to reflect on how they responded to the poems as well as the situations depicted in each chapter.

Photography is a component of my self-care, a hobby that relaxes and renews me. All of the photographs included were taken with my first digital camera, a gift to myself when I completed the Master of Arts in Pastoral Theology degree.

Following the narratives is information about the photographs, including where they were shot and my reason for choosing each as a visual representation of the *be-attitudes.*

The final entry is a suggested reading list of books and articles that encourage, provide support for, and enhance the meaning of this holy work called chaplaincy. These references have not only profoundly influenced my chaplaincy they have also sustained me during the creative process of authoring *The Be-Attitudes of Chaplaincy.*

It is my heartfelt prayer that I have honored the courageous people whose narratives are shared here. I am forever grateful for the opportunity to birth their sacred stories and for the blessings I received from being with each of them. My personal journey through life and my chaplain ministry are profoundly richer for the trust each placed in me. I hope that you find inspiration and encouragement for your own journey in the stories and reflections you are about to read.

Chapter One

Be Called

I have called you by name; you are mine.

- Isaiah 43:1

Delicate dawn light
fingering its way through majestic tree branches.
Playful squirrels awakening,
perhaps by a chorus of birds
frolicking limb to limb,
pausing momentarily
nibbling at new buds.
Blushing tomatoes
ripe for picking
shamelessly beckoning
from an otherwise green garden.
Morning doves
cooing to each other
from undetectable locations.
Creation
participating in the Call.

Participating in the Call

Our calling is where our deepest gladness and the world's hunger meet.
- Frederick Buechner

I am a *Spiritual Midwife*. I help birth Sacred Stories. This is the ministry to which God called me. It just took many years and the gentle nudge from a dying close friend for me to turn my head toward the still, small voice. The concept of calling is strange like that. We need to be close enough to the sweet spot of the caller to truly hear. Sometimes we hear at the first sound, sometimes we wander around a while before hearing a call that sounds familiar, and sometimes we are called many, many times. Like a determined parent, God as Caller is nothing if not persistent.

When I was a youngster, family members used their voices to gain my attention and draw me home, often for reasons known to them but not to me…yet. Literal calling was accomplished by shouting out the most familiar thing to me—my name. If I was nearby, callers only had to raise their voices somewhat above normal for the desired outcome. However, if I was outside in the yard, one of my brothers or my mother might open the front door and call my name in a louder than normal tone. There were times when I roamed off with friends a little beyond my boundaries and out of sight. When called, a few neighbors would hear my name and let me know I was being summoned home. Voice decibel levels grew exponentially with the distance I was away from home. Occasionally, one of my brothers was sent to find me because I was out of sight at a friend's house or at the park. My brother would shout my name while walking in the direction he thought I might be, hoping I would eventually hear him and start my homeward journey before he had trekked all the way to where I was.

We need to be close enough to the sweet spot of the caller to truly hear.

If I heard my name being called and did not quickly respond with "Coming," patience waned on the part of my caller and I knew I would have some explaining to do when we finally connected. My brother might not only complain when he found me, but he might also express his frustration to our parents.

My unique position as the only daughter in a houseful of sons did not exempt me from being obedient. Early in childhood, I learned that I needed to pay attention. Just like my brothers, I was responsible for listening and responding when my name was called and for moving quickly toward whoever was calling me. In those days one came when called.

Over time, calling methodologies have changed, but families continue to use escalating tones and words to call their children home for dinner or to complete some unfinished task. Cell phones now save our voice boxes, text messages offer the use of capital letters and exclamation points for evoking a sense of urgency or frustration, and social media offers more visual methods for calling out to and personally connecting with others. We humans continue to call each other in myriad ways.

Spiritual calling by God seems similar to literal callings between human beings. For example, God's ways of calling are also personal and varied. "I have called you by name; you are mine" (Isaiah 43:1). Does the call of God invite us to be attentive, listen, and respond? If we are not anticipating or listening for it, do we simply miss the beckoning "still, small voice"? What about distance from God? If the further from home we move, the more difficult it is for us to hear our parent when we are called, then could the same be said for spiritual distance? Does being in a state of spiritual awareness heighten our receptivity to being called and detecting a call on our life?

> *What does it mean to be called by God? How do we know when we are being called?*

What does it mean to be called by God? How do we know when we are being called? Can we improve our spiritual hearing? Is it possible that God calls us to a specific vocation early in life, only to call again later when we least expect it? Does each call, response, and experience prepare and strengthen us for the next call in such a way that our life experiences become like a well-tended garden in full bloom? Is this the way we become what we were created to be?

An artist friend of mine used to paint exquisite portraits of children and adults. Walking into Ellie's studio one day, I admired her many works of art hanging on the walls. When I complimented Ellie on her extraordinary gift, she softly whispered, "The *desire* is the gift." Reflecting on my own life, I have often wondered if I, perhaps like everyone else, arrived in this world with a seedling *gift of desire* tucked away deep in my spirit. Is that *desire* my calling? Does it happen that over time the tiny seedling desire either grows and blossoms in full glory from attention and nurture or withers from neglect? My seedling call to chaplaincy came when I least expected it. Through the years, I had many gardeners watering, weeding, and radiating the sunlight of encouragement.

When I think about the idea of being called to chaplaincy and consider the path that brought me to this point, I am aware how frequently I am asked, "How did you *decide* to become a chaplain?" The answer is neither short nor simple, but I usually reply by describing the process as feeling like God has been gently tugging on my sleeve for years, whispering softly, "Jo, can we talk?" However, instead of checking in, I was busy establishing a career and earning quite a decent living in the world of computer technology. That profession served me well for over twenty years. It provided the means to purchase a lovely home where I raised my daughter and years later also experienced the joy of grandchildren toddling around. Life was good. I could not have predicted all this was about to change with one late-night telephone call. The call I dreaded came shortly after midnight, telling me that my best friend, Judy, had died. She was just forty-four years old. Breast cancer had taken Judy's life, and the grief of losing her rocked my world!

Judy and I became neighbors when I moved into the house next door. We each had one child. Before long, our daughters became inseparable. Little girls who loved to play dress-up, ride bicycles, finger paint, and climb trees were drawn to each other. Neighbors often referred to them as "the towhead and the redhead." They played incessantly while their mothers watched from the sidelines.

One of the few things I knew about Judy was her love of *The Price Is Right* television game show. She had frequently expressed a desire to be a contestant, confident she would "win big" if given the opportunity. Then one cool-weather holiday when Judy and I were both home with windows wide open, I heard her holler loudly, "Judy, come on down! You're the next contestant on *The Price Is Right*!" I laughed so hard she couldn't help but hear me. A brief teasing conversation through open windows about her love of that particular game show was the spark needed to ignite a longstanding friendship. God called two women together through a game show host shouting out at contestants in a tiny television studio. That day, Bob Barker hosting *The Price Is Right* reached far beyond his studio audience. I remember thinking God sure does work in mysterious ways.

Our mothers-next-door experience lasted a mere eighteen months before the death of Judy's father drew her home to Abilene to comfort and care for her mother. We may have been neighbors for only a brief moment in time, but the seeds of an enduring friendship had been planted. Eighteen months gave our friendship roots sturdy enough to sustain us through twenty-two years of joys, sorrows, and three hundred dusty West Texas miles. We talked by telephone often, and dreaded, but occasionally drove, the tedious five-hour drive between Amarillo and Abilene. We often remarked about the wonderful way our friendship clicked. If I was feeling down about some life challenge, Judy was up and could lift my spirit just by talking to her. The next time the phone rang, it might be Judy who needed a lift. Our friendship was deep and reciprocal. My relationship with Judy was the closest experience to having a sister I would ever know.

My relationship with Judy was the closest experience to having a sister I would ever know.

Judy and I thought raising teen-age daughters was the most difficult trial two mothers could face. Then one dreadful day in November, Judy told me she had just been diagnosed with breast cancer. Her delightful sense of humor and ability to "find the funny" (as she called it) in nearly any serious situation was one of Judy's many treasured qualities. She joked about how having a mastectomy was going to help chisel her down to a more svelte size. I laughed as I always did at Judy's humor, but I could barely contain the waves of grief sweeping over me. I hung up the phone with tears trickling down my cheeks and then broke into uncontrollable mournful sobs.

Judy underwent surgery, followed by months of chemotherapy. Sometimes I would surprise her by showing up at one of those treatments to hold her hand and take her to lunch afterward. Judy amazed me with her determination, stamina, and strong faith. She lived in the moment, boldly denying cancer the chance to define her life. Before long, Judy heard the news that her cancer was in remission. We celebrated in her favorite way: prayerful thanksgiving, shopping, and eating.

Two short years later, Judy's cancer returned, this time with a vengeance. Nothing seemed to slow it down. Chemotherapy and radiation could not prevent the cancer from metastasizing to her bones. One of my most vivid memories is when Judy and I met at her daughter's new home between Dallas and Ft. Worth for a girls' weekend. I slept on the sofa bed in the living room and woke in the morning to a light streaming from the kitchen. When I turned toward that light, I saw Judy in her nightgown at the kitchen sink, her shiny, slick, bald head almost glowing in the bluish fluorescent light. Prior to then, Judy had been determined not to let anyone see her without a wig. I laid there and watched, tears sliding down the tip of my nose and dripping onto the pillow. Judy was methodically swallowing her morning medications, unaware I was awake. Before she could notice me, I turned my head away from the kitchen and sobbed into the pillow as I began to grasp the force of grief welling up inside me. That was the first time I considered my dear friend might die. My feelings ran the gamut between indescribable sadness for the physical suffering Judy was experiencing and anger that cancer was taking her from me.

Shortly thereafter, Judy told me she wanted to stop the cancer treatments, and she pleaded for my support with her decision. She was an intelligent woman, who asked her oncologist the difficult questions and weighed her options. Treatment would provide a few extra months, not cure her cancer. Naturally, the women in Judy's family—her mother, sister, and daughter—were all encouraging her to continue with chemotherapy. As we talked privately, I heard my precious friend express her battle fatigue, desire for quality of life in her remaining time on earth, steadfast faith in God, and her assurance of eternal life. I love Judy's family and completely resonated with their longing to keep her with us as long as possible. But my love for Judy trumped all other feelings. I promised to support her decision. I also promised to help in any way I could with her family's disappointment.

Under hospice care for the last few months of her life, Judy taught me how to "live into death." She spoke those words as a way of letting her family and friends understand her philosophy of dying. Judy often said she could "die into it or live into it." This was her way of expressing the difference between giving up in despair and letting go with acceptance. Judy chose to live every minute right to the very end. Just four weeks before she died, as we sat in the park near her home, Judy suggested I "do something for hospice" to honor our friendship after her death. When I inquired if she wanted me to make a donation, Judy simply said, "You'll know what to do." I promised her I would "do something" and Judy promised to "send butterflies" to let me know she was forever with me in spirit.

> *She promised to "send butterflies" to let me know she was forever with me in spirit.*

During the long drive home to Amarillo from Abilene, I recall thinking a donation would probably be the best solution. I was fairly certain there was no hospice center in

Amarillo. Was I ever wrong! Much to my surprise, there was a twenty-four-bed, stand-alone hospice center, which still exists today. At the time, it was affiliated with St. Anthony's Hospital. For well over two years I managed to avoid the hands-on work there. I was supervising twenty computer programmers and working ridiculously long hours. Every time I noticed an advertisement in the paper for an evening training of hospice volunteers, I used my career, home, and first-born grandchild as reasons to avoid that persistent spiritual tugging on my sleeve. And I was still grieving the loss of my best friend. The thought of being around other dying people rekindled my sadness of losing Judy's presence and friendship. I missed her more than I could express.

Making a donation would have been the easy path. But for some reason I felt giving money was not the "knowing" Judy had predicted. I kept remembering my promise to "do something." And there was that ever-growing, persistent sensation of a tugging on my sleeve. Two and a half years after Judy's death, I noticed an advertisement in the paper for a Saturday training session for hospice volunteers. It was time to commit and fulfill my promise to a faithful friend.

A female staff chaplain trained me and about five others to be volunteers at the hospice center. Every Tuesday evening, I dependably reported to the front desk, where I watched the closed circuit monitor for visitors at the door, permitted entrance to families and friends of patients, answered the telephone, and occasionally washed a few dirty coffee cups left in the kitchen. About a month into this, my boredom grew exponentially with the waning evening hours as visitors and incoming telephone calls subsided. I began wandering the halls, noticing patients who were still awake and, more importantly, those who were alone.

As I sat listening to patients, I noticed stories birthing in those hospice rooms. I recall a young Buddhist patient dying of AIDS, an elderly grandmother of ten, and a very young boy dying with a rare kidney disease. This was the beginning of my calling as a Spiritual Midwife. Although I was only slightly aware of my burgeoning call, as days passed, my realization grew, and I knew this was the start of a new and deeply meaningful journey.

As days passed, I began to realize this was the beginning of a new and meaningful journey.

Patients, families, and staff began singing my praises to the hospice chaplain who had trained me. She telephoned to assess my interest in becoming a volunteer chaplain. I was confused by her question. What is a volunteer chaplain? I thought to myself. As we talked, I became more and more curious about volunteer chaplaincy. I discovered I would need two additional days of training with some collaborative follow-up and decided to go forward with this opportunity. After the training sessions, I added some Saturday hours to my volunteer schedule, took on visitation to hospice patients in two local nursing homes, and within six months found myself researching full-time chaplaincy on the Internet. My volunteer ministry was rapidly becoming more meaningful to me than my salaried vocation.

While some hospices and hospitals utilize volunteer chaplains, most require their salaried staff chaplains be board certified. One evening, as I sat at my computer researching what was necessary to make the transition from being a volunteer chaplain to becoming a full-time, salaried, board-certified chaplain, I felt that old familiar tug on my sleeve stronger than ever. As I paused to finally give the tug some serious consideration, it seemed God said, "Now that I have your attention, can we talk?"

That night, I argued with God. Pointing to the evidence on my computer, I reminded God that to become a board-certified chaplain I would need to leave a high-paying job, obtain a Master's Degree in Theology or a Master of Divinity degree (M.Div.), locate a hospital offering a good Clinical Pastoral Education (CPE) program, apply, be accepted, and successfully complete four units of CPE, sell my home where I had lived for nearly twenty years, leave my family, and trust I would be hired as a chaplain when I finished. Oh yes, and I was over fifty years old! That long list seemed like a logical rebuttal. But all I could hear was a reverberating, "Sell everything, give to the poor, and come follow me" (paraphrase of Matthew 19:21; Mark 10:21; Luke 18:22).

The next day as I was mowing the front lawn, a gorgeous orange and black monarch butterfly persistently followed my movements. Giving in to the beauty and intrigued by its flight pattern around me, I stopped the mower and sat down on the front step. Though the butterfly never landed on me, she continued to gracefully fly around me. I was mesmerized. After several minutes, she lit on a flower in the garden under my window. Eventually, she took off soaring over my house. I wrote in my butterfly journal: I wonder if Judy is affirming my tug toward chaplaincy?

I wrote in my butterfly journal: I wonder if Judy is affirming my tug toward chaplaincy?

For a time, I questioned why I wasn't called to chaplaincy when I was younger and more robust. The answer came back quickly and resolutely, "You weren't ready." After that, all I saw were Judy's butterflies, and all I could sense was God saying, "You can do this."

Deciding to become a chaplain was less of a conscious *decision* to do it and more of a deep *knowing* I could not *NOT* do it. The rest is history. The time, energy, and dedication it took to accomplish the necessary requirements were nothing in light of the spiritual energy above, below, and around drawing me onward.

Rev. Jenny Lannom, my CPE supervisor at Presbyterian Hospital in Albuquerque, New Mexico said she wished she could "bottle my zeal." I truly enjoyed the CPE program that was teaching me how to channel my zeal. I loved the work on my Master's degree, the clinical work, and the ministry of "allowing God to wear my face," as Thomas Merton once said. Since the beginning, every room I enter and every patient I encounter leaves me with an overwhelming sense of humility. I am honored by their trust in me to be a sacred vessel into which they birth their stories. When strangers ask me what a chaplain is, I respond simply: I am a *Spiritual Midwife*. I help birth Sacred Stories.

Calls come as lower-case "c" or upper-case "C" calls, and I imagine they appear frequently throughout our lives. I equate the many callings of God to something like opening a mailbox at home to find it jam-packed with invitations to parties, activities, events, and even vocations. If we slow down long enough to listen for the "still, small voice" of God beckoning, there just might be a summons to serve as a chaplain.

God certainly utilized every available method to gain my attention. When I began paying closer attention to friends' advice about getting out from behind my desk and computer to “let my light shine” (as one friend offered); when I listened to coworkers say they counted on me as a trusted confidant; when I heard friends suggest I might be good in a field requiring listening skills; and when butterfly sightings began to fill the pages of my journal, I finally tuned into and turned toward the God who had been patiently tugging on my sleeve.

Frequently, I think about how much I love Judy and miss her presence in my life. Being unable to pick up the telephone, call, and hear her voice used to make me feel as if I had lost her forever. Sometimes, when I am missing Judy most, I sigh and reflect on all the ways our friendship continues to be a vessel into which God pours abundant blessings, cascading over and saturating me to this day—years after her death. Once I thought a call to chaplaincy was my gift to Judy. Now it seems crystal clear this gift of chaplaincy is as deep and reciprocal as our friendship. Like ripples from a rock tossed gently into a quiet lake, my call and response to chaplaincy are special gifts from Judy flowing from the center of her love. She gives to me day after day...without ceasing.

I continue to make sighting entries in my butterfly journal—each butterfly a reminder of my sister and precious friend Judy—and an affirmation of my call to become a Spiritual Midwife.

Calling Prayer:

Source of Universal Life,

Are you calling from the moment of birth, or have you implanted the seed of desire for your purpose, as I was knitted together in my mother's womb? Is the *seed of my calling* blossoming in frustration or nurtured by the loving waters of supportive family and friends recognizing the gift within? If you are calling me to chaplaincy, may I not hesitate, but instead respond *with gentle curiosity* to all the ways you seek to gain my attention and speak to my heart.

Persistent Hound of Heaven, *awaken my* longings to the needs and hunger of the world that I might recognize the cries of the *hopeful* and the hopeless, newborn and elderly, pampered and *neglected*, those fighting for life and the suicidal, the godly and godless. Grant me *ears to hear* their silent cries, hands strong enough to hold their pain, *and give me a heart tender enough to care for each one as Imago Dei.* Amen.

Reflective Questions:

- What images does the phrase *spiritual midwife* evoke in you?
- What is the deepest desire of your heart?
- To what is that desire calling you?
- What family members, friends, and colleagues have watered the seeds of your calling? How are you responding?
- Was there a feeling of resistance and what was that like? From where was the resistance coming? How have you moved through the resistance, if you have? If you have not moved through the resistance, what are you doing to seek guidance?
- If you responded to the call of chaplaincy, *re-call* your first meaningful experience as a chaplain that filled you with both wonder and an overwhelming affirmation you were exactly where you were called to be.

Blessed are the poor in spirit,
for they open their hearts
to your call

Chapter Two

Be Prepared

When the student is ready, the teacher will appear.

- Mabel Collins

Call it *ready* when parched earth softens
under late summer raindrops.

Call it *able* when a crafty cat leaps
to perch on a fence top.

Call it *arranged* when a music score opens
an audience's expectant ears.

Call it *predisposed* when a keen-eyed eagle swoops
to grasp unaware prey.

Call it *prepped* when spring farmland enfolds
delicate seedlings.

Call it *primed* when a dry well gushes
forth life-giving water.

Call it *rehearsed* when ancient oaks turn
vibrant shades of crimson.

Call it *capable* when the Master Artist paints
peach-colored sunsets.

Prepared

We are not human beings having a spiritual experience;
we are spiritual beings having a human experience.
- Pierre Teilhard de Chardin

Many years ago, I made a pilgrimage of sorts to a place that took my breath away. My parents, who loved driving and teaching us about the extraordinary and varied landscape of America, took their four young children to the South Rim of the Grand Canyon. Although my memory of that arduous trip has many gaps, the Grand Canyon left an unrepentant reverberation echoing in my soul. Decades later, I was presented with a serendipitous gift and returned to the Grand Canyon in early fall—this time to the North Rim. The trip felt like a pilgrimage, allowing me to open up to whatever I had left there as a child and respond to what the Grand Canyon had planted within me. Wanting to capture every moment of the journey, I enthusiastically logged my experiences in a daily journal.

Visiting the North Rim involves patience and commitment. Driving from Texas takes two extra days of travel—one day in and another to drive out. Travelers willing to make the journey are well-rewarded with scenery vastly different from the South Rim. A winding road deceptively carved through outstretched meadow creates a fascinating illusion of uniformity. Because the North Rim receives double the rain and snowfall of the South Rim, its landscape contains towering pines and massive aspens. By late September, heart-shaped leaves on white-trunked aspens turn vibrant gold and orange as they wave, welcoming passersby. Even the Kaibab squirrels scampering through the dense forest are different. North Rim squirrels look more like skunks with wide white elongated stripes down their backs.

> *This time the trip felt like a pilgrimage, allowing me to open up to whatever I had left there as a child and respond to what the Grand Canyon had planted within me.*

As I approached the Lodge to check in to one of the extremely rustic cabins, my heart cracked wide open. I felt a wild combination of awe and intimidation unfolding and exposing my masked vulnerability. I stood mesmerized; wondering if this was how Native Americans felt when they first encountered the majesty and mystery of the Grand Canyon. Were they humbled, as I was, standing on the precipice of this vast gorge etched by an enduring river flow?

With spiritual experiences of the North Rim accumulating, entry upon entry in my journal became laden with attempts at unearthing adequate words and photographs to describe my feelings. Then, unexpectedly, on the third day of snapping pictures, I overheard a young boy, about five years old, excitedly shout out, "*Uff da*!" As a woman of Scandinavian descent, I immediately recognized this Norwegian expression of sensory overload. That was it! My senses were overloaded by the magnificence of this sacred place: the vastness of the river-carved canyon, the ever-changing light reflecting on layers of red rock, the sweet fragrance of pinion trees, and glorious, indescribable sunsets. Moment by moment my senses soaked up the grandeur. And I was humbled, deeply humbled, in the presence of creation's mystery before me.

Sitting on the North Rim Lodge balcony the night before leaving, my sense of humility intensified as I witnessed one more gift of this extraordinary ancient canyon. With the sinking sun illuminating billowy clouds in the southwestern sky, an exotic lightning dance across the abyss on the South Rim held my undivided attention for hours. Sojourners from around the world sat side-by-side in the stillness of the evening air, each seemingly stirred by the awesome truth of a greater Presence before us. At some point, a warm, gentle breeze kissed my cheeks, as if waking me from a dream I hoped would never end.

I thought about Celtic "thin places" where the divide between human and divine narrows.

As I stood and turned to leave, I thought about Celtic "thin places," where a person experiences only a slight divide between heaven and earth, between human and divine: Here on the North Rim of the Grand Canyon is one of my thin places, where I am unmasked, sense my oneness with creation, and am transformed. Here my ego falls away. I experience openness and receptivity. Here my heart, mind, body, and spirit become malleable. Here I am laid open, ready, prepared...for all that awaits me.

This was the exact spirit of openness I hoped to carry into my clinical training to become a skilled chaplain. I would need to lean fully into my supervisor's classroom teachings, fellow student chaplains' shared experiences, and clinical pastoral visits with patients, families, and staff, allowing my spirit to be transformed by each. I was there to learn and the standard competencies used to assess and evaluate my process at the conclusion of each of four units would reflect my progress.

Clinical Pastoral Education (CPE) is a year-long residency program of formation. I was not certain what to expect, but I was fairly confident my year in Albuquerque would be fashioned by much more than three hundred sixty-five days checked off my Ansel Adams calendar. I did not tiptoe timidly into the program. I plunged headlong with the only other speed I knew besides reverse. I thought I was ready for anything.

Just seven days into the program, I timidly walked onto the oncology unit at Presbyterian Hospital. This was my training ground. This was the primary assignment for my year as a chaplain resident. This was the clinical duty I was hired for and had agreed to perform. This was scarier than I anticipated. Gently, I knocked on the windowless door of a patient's room on the oncology unit. I was making a "cold call." No one referred the patient in this room to me. I just printed a census report for my assigned unit, reviewed the list as if I had insight about what all the abbreviations meant, took a deep breath, convinced myself to give it my best, mustered courage from the very depths of my soul, and pressed on, firmly believing every pastoral visit would prepare me for the next one.

When I heard a faint invitation to enter, I opened the door to find a Latino man in his late thirties or early forties alone in the room with nary a sign of recent visitors. There were no greeting cards on the windowsill, no visitor clothes crumpled on the chair, no television turned on, and no one in the room but the patient in the bed. His large liquid brown eyes peered over the bedrails as I entered the room. I swept the room with a quick glance, apprehensively approached his hospital bed, and introduced myself as "Chaplain Jo." Mr. Q's huge brown eyes instantly opened to twice their normal size. He leaned toward me on his elbow and with fear in his voice like I had never heard before, loudly cried, "Am I going to die?"

Mr. Q's response shocked me as much as my

presence in the room startled him. As I moved closer to his bed, I saw Mr. Q's hands trembling and raw terror in his eyes. I could not imagine how my simple introduction would have generated such fear. All I wanted was to run out the door, but basic human compassion told me I needed to do something quickly to calm his anxiety. I promptly began fumbling for the words to soothe his nerves. I said something like, "Oh Mr. Q, I'm so sorry I upset you. I'm just making my rounds this morning. The hospital does not send chaplains to deliver that kind of information. I'm just part of your support team." Mr. Q was not convinced. "Are you sure?" he retorted. My stomach was doing back-flips, and my mind was racing, jumping back and forth between thoughts of how to reduce Mr. Q's anxiety and what to do with my own. Feelings of inadequacy welled up in my gut. Although I could hardly wait to get out of his room, I knew I could not leave until Mr. Q became more settled. Our dialogue continued for over twenty minutes, alternating between my apologetic posture and his gradually diminishing fear.

I could not imagine how my simple introduction would have generated such fear.

Ultimately, the answers to all my questions came through processing this and future pastoral visits with mentors and implementing the skills taught in CPE; however, early in the program I was also coming to grips with my own "growing edges." These were (and still are) places within me that get tweaked by various encounters and produce less than graceful inward and/or outward responses. My use of the words "chaplain shoes" weaves throughout my CPE journal notes as an indication of my growing edges. Right from the beginning of my CPE residency year, I associated my level of comfort or discomfort with breaking in a pair of new shoes. My awkward visit with Mr. Q left me feeling unprepared to be a chaplain and afraid to share my feelings of inadequacy with anyone. I was fearful of being judged. My journal entry that day reads, "These chaplain shoes seem like they belong to someone else today because they sure don't feel comfortable on me...I'm probably the only one feeling this way."

Actually, I was not the only one feeling awkward, unskilled, and unprepared. Each of the seven chaplain residents in my CPE group expressed similar feelings, stating they felt as though they were "playing dress-up" as they tried to look, feel, and present themselves as chaplains. Relieved to hear I was not alone in my feelings, I still had to contend with wanting to be a skillful chaplain—immediately.

CPE is an inward as well as outward journey. Competency in the field of chaplaincy is so much more than honing a few skills. Success in the CPE program would require me to hold a mirror up to everything I cherished, believed, and knew to be true about myself. Although CPE did not necessarily demand I change my personal truths; it did, however, invite and encourage me to be changed by various life experiences. Under the observant eyes of an Association of Clinical Pastoral Education (ACPE) certified supervisor, I could safely reflect on how I was affected by a variety of pastoral encounters with people in crisis. Within the confines of this teaching program, I was afforded copious opportunities to assess what gets triggered inside me when a full-term baby is delivered stillborn, a mother leans over to kiss her adult son good-bye as he takes his last breath, an infant drowns, a child is diagnosed with cancer, a mother asks to have her newborn blessed, or a family extends the invitation to officiate the funeral of their loved one. Through intense theological and personal reflection on my experiences and those of the other students, I learned I was my own best instrument for being present as a chaplain in the midst of suffering.

Day by day, visit by visit, my "chaplain shoes" became more and more comfortable.

Because memories of my first pastoral visit linger like a familiar melody, I often reflect upon what I learned from time spent with Mr. Q. In addition to the general pastoral skill of introducing myself somewhat differently—I now introduce myself as part of the patient's support team, *followed by* name and title—I also understand the multi-layered components of pastoral care. Mr. Q had several attitudes about clergy impacting his response to me that day. In subsequent visits with Mr. Q (yes, I mustered the courage to go back), I learned that he believed hospital chaplains only visited to deliver bad news, but even more importantly, Mr. Q knew he had cancer and was terrified of dying. When a chaplain dropped by, his intense fear of dying escalated to nearly unmanageable anxiety. Mr. Q's anxiety and my nervousness about his feeling anxious collided head-on that day. Subsequently, I learned a valuable lesson about my internal and external responses to feeling challenged: My voice tightens, my posture becomes defensive, and my words become apologetic. Ensuing pastoral visits solidified my newfound awareness; however, it was the initial visit with Mr. Q that motivated me to set one of my first unit CPE goals. Finding my voice would be a focus over the next twelve weeks—possibly the rest of my life—and Mr. Q was the catalyst for doing so.

Opportunities to learn and grow in CPE are abundant. When I approached CPE with a spirit of curiosity and awe, I learned skills through clinical supervision, academic study, and the richness of hands-on practice. Because no two situations are exactly the same, no two pastoral visits are identical. Being humbly present to an assortment of family systems and values, diverse ethnic populations, and innumerable expressions of spirituality expanded my practical knowledge for relating to people in crisis—people who are quite possibly at their most vulnerable.

A key component continues to be the balance between confidence and humility. Confidence in my ability to step into any situation, assess the spiritual atmosphere and needs, be an instrument of conflict resolution, and work collaboratively with the medical team took root during my CPE residency and grew with each encounter. Increasing confidence correlates with the level of comfort I feel in my chaplain shoes.

During my year-long residency, I purchased several pair of shoes trying to find a pair so perfectly comfortable that my feet would not ache at the end of the day. After twenty-plus years of sitting behind a computer, walking the halls of a 600-bed hospital made my feet scream for relief. I remember keeping a bottle of water in the freezer so I could alternate rolling it under each bare foot when I arrived home. Doing this one evening early in my residency, I smiled through the pain as I made a mental comparison between literal and figurative comfort in my chaplain shoes. My feet were adjusting to a new rhythm and routine, just like my mind and spirit. Eventually, my feet adjusted to the hours of walking, regardless of the actual shoes I chose to wear. And ultimately, an ever-growing pastoral proficiency increased my self-confidence, making

Humility in pastoral care entails remembering God is present before I arrive.

my figurative chaplain shoes feel as if I was born in them.

On the other hand, humility in pastoral care entails remembering God is present long before I arrive on the scene. Every room is holy ground and every patient carries sacred stories. When I approach them with awe and humility, patients frequently place confidence and trust in me to help birth, hold, and protect the story gestating on that particular day. I once stood in awe of the Grand Canyon's grandeur. I now stand in daily awe of an ongoing process where I am a trusted participant in birth, death, and the tenacity of the human spirit. Pastoral care visits are "thin places" where separation between divine and human is almost imperceptible.

Preparation Prayer:

Omniscient One,

I ponder daily and *pray unceasingly* about this service of holy trust to which you have called me. I knock, I seek, I ask and *I await* the embrace of *your potter's hands* to mold and make of me a sacred vessel. *Teach me* how to witness a final breath. *Guide me* in the ways to hold a mother's tears. *Grant me wisdom* to release a soul to you.

Touch the hollows of my heart with your warm compassion, *fill me* to overflowing with your unconditional love, *prepare me* to be a reflection of your abiding spirit, and *expand my* often unyielding *spirit. Transform me into a spacious container* that I might carry back to you the tears of joy and of sorrow. May the holiness of our tears water and bring forth new life. *Empty me to begin again.* Amen.

Reflective Questions:

- Quiet yourself for a few minutes and reflect on a time when you felt humbled by a place or a person. Write down any feelings you experienced.
- When did you have a life experience that stopped you in your tracks for your inability to know what to do? Write about it.
- Reflect on what the word *formation* means to you.
- What are your strengths? How might your strengths provide a basis for chaplaincy?
- What are your growing edges? What might your growing edges reveal?
- What are you doing to "grow yourself"?
- Consider reading The Wounded Healer by Henri Nouwen.
- If you have a spiritual director or faith companion, spend some time with that person in dialogue about your strengths as well as your growing edges.
- If you do not have a spiritual director or faith companion, give consideration to finding and establishing a relationship with one.
- If you are currently a chaplain, when did you last process an unnerving pastoral visit with your own spiritual director or faith companion? In what ways was that debriefing process helpful?

Blessed are the meek,

for they are humbled in formation.

Chapter Three

Be Present

May we have the grace to be God's Presence in the world by our companionship, our sharing, our unconditional love, and the gift of ourselves in service to others.

- Celeste Cotter, CSJ

Expectantly, we

beg God to speak,

plead with God for miracles,

demand proof of God's existence,

seek God's touch.

Frequently, we

fail to notice

(because the packaging is different than expected?)

thunder rumble in a rainstorm,

a newborn's sweet scent,

stars flame out across a midnight sky,

a butterfly brush past.

Presence

A man prayed, and at first, he thought that prayer was talking. But he became more and more quiet until in the end he realized prayer is listening.
- Soren Kierkegaard

Back in 2004, I watched a movie titled *Shall We Dance*. My interest in the movie was spawned by the casting of Susan Sarandon and Richard Gere in the lead roles. There are many poignant scenes and memorable lines in this movie; however, one in particular lingers. In a scene where Susan Sarandon's character, Beverly, offers her perspective on why people get married, she suggests that in marriage relationships, we promise to care about everything every day. Beverly concludes with, "You're saying [to your spouse], 'Your life will not go unnoticed because I will notice it. Your life will not go un-witnessed because I will be your witness.'"

Powerful words: *I will be your witness*. Yet, isn't that exactly what we do in every authentic relationship? We bear witness to another's life one snippet, one moment, one encounter at a time. Over the course of a lifetime, we may witness a birth, a marriage, a crime, or a death. If we witness an accident or crime, we may be expected to recall details based on our observations of the event. Being a witness carries a certain level of responsibility; however, witnessing a life can be as basic as being present and listening.

When I "Google" the word *listen*, over a billion references appear on the Internet. There is even the *International Listening Association* based in Minnesota. Amazon carries over twelve thousand book titles with the word *listen*. Active listening is the subject of seminars, retreats, books, movies, and countless research articles. One could even speculate that the human body is designed for listening. When I taught Sunday school, at the beginning of each year, I asked my first grade students how many ears and how many mouths we have. Of course, they shouted out "two" and "one," respectively. Then, when I proposed that God must want us to listen twice as much as we speak, their looks of puzzlement were priceless. Years later, as a novice chaplain resident, my first unit of CPE was devoted to the topic of active listening, and my experiences provided fertile ground for honing the skills of listening, witnessing, and being present.

Ministry to oncology patients and their families is remarkably relational. Oncology staff, including the chaplain, regularly gets to know patients on a deep level. This is true for several reasons. When patients are diagnosed with cancer, they often become more reflective about their mortality. These patients can also be hospitalized quite frequently, depending on the types of chemotherapy administered and their physical responses to treatment. Similarities tend to end there because every patient's personal narrative is unique. Occasionally, I meet a patient whose story gives me pause. Stuart was one of those patients.

When I first met Stuart, I was convinced he had no interest in speaking with a chaplain. He was alone in his room with the lights dimmed and shades pulled down. As my eyes adjusted to the minimal light, I noticed Stuart had a rather scraggly beard, and his longish hair appeared to be matted, making his age difficult to discern. He was polite but not very responsive to what I thought were creatively-formed reflective questions. After a few minutes and several attempts to engage Stuart, I offered my contact information and concluded the pastoral visit. Later as I charted my initial spiritual assessment of him, one of the words I used in describing Stuart was "disengaged." Because there were many other patients on the unit to visit, I moved on.

> *Occasionally, I meet a patient whose story gives me pause. Stuart was one of those patients.*

Three days later, I received a page from the oncology charge nurse, Angela. When I arrived on the unit, Angela advised me that Stuart had taken a significant turn for the worse. We talked briefly about Stuart's lack of interest in having people in his room and Angela assured me his attitude had not changed. Stuart did not even like it when the nurses came in his room but tolerated their presence for the pain relief medications they provided. Angela reminded me she had no expectation that I would visit Stuart. She just thought I would like to know he was considerably sicker today.

My first thought was of the nurses caring for Stuart. Even if he had not related to them, the nurses cared about Stuart and would be affected by his death. Nurse Gabby had cared for Stuart during the three days he had been hospitalized thus far. I searched and found her at the blanket warmer reaching inside to grab one for Stuart. Turning toward me, Gabby's eyes were watery with imminent tears. She shared her sorrow about witnessing a patient in the final stage of life, especially one who seemed to carry so much unspoken sadness inside. After ministering to Gabby, who needed to express her personal grief, I quietly vowed to attempt another visit with Stuart sometime later that day.

With the day winding down, I reviewed my notes. I noticed a circle around Stuart's room number and a hand-scrawled note reminding me to see him. Glancing at the clock, I realized it was nearing my scheduled departure time. For just a second or two, I contemplated putting off this visit until the next day. I also recall wondering what was causing me to delay seeing Stuart. I briefly considered that my feelings of resistance were due to fear of rejection or dismissal. At a deeper level, I also knew if Stuart died before I had a chance to attempt another visit, the feelings I had to process would be significantly compounded.

Mustering my inner courage, I arrived at Stuart's door, knocked gently, and waited for an invitation to enter. When none came, I briefly considered his non-answer a justification for leaving. But I knew better. When I opened the door, light from the hall streamed into the room, falling on Stuart's disheveled hair. Immediately, I re-introduced myself and asked if it would be okay to come in and just sit with him for a while. Stuart groaned a bit, and I told him I would take that as a "yes." I pulled the empty visitor chair up next to his bed and sat very close to his head so I could hear if he chose to talk. Since Stuart said nothing, I began to speak.

> *I pulled the empty visitor chair up next to his bed and sat close to his head so I could hear him talk. He chose not to.*

Stuart lay silently in the bed with his eyes closed. I spoke softly about all the things I had to offer such as music of his choice, reading, or praying for him. No response. Half expecting Stuart to remind me of my promise to "just sit with him," I whispered that I was going to breathe with him for a while. Then I became quiet. All I could hear in the room was the gentle flow of my breath and the faint movement of air through Stuart's beard. Presence, I thought to myself. This is being present.

There was such stillness in the room that I barely noticed Stuart's left hand reach through the bed rail, turn, and open, palm up. Greatly surprised by the gesture, I hesitated for a moment and he began to withdraw his hand. I reached out, put my hand in Stuart's, palms together, and wrapped my thumb around his. He squeezed my hand gently in acknowledgment, and then said, "I'm scared."

In whispered tones, Stuart shared his story. I listened intently. Stuart's life was memorable, mainly for his ability to survive. Childhood and adulthood were marred by abuse, struggle, and suffering. Stuart had made several irreversible young adult decisions. Although he altered his path, a cloud of bad luck stubbornly hung overhead. Living much of his adult life on the streets, sleep deprivation and survival became Stuart's constant companions. Prior to beginning his narrative, Stuart had inquired about my keeping his personal story confidential. I now understood why. Stuart trusted no one.

Stillness hovered in the room again and I wondered if I had taken him in a direction he did not wish to go.

Considerable time passed, but because Stuart had entrusted his story to me, I wanted to be sure he had shared all he intended to share. At some point, I gently reminded him of his opening statement about being scared and asked if he were more afraid of life or death. Stillness ominously hovered in the room again, and I wondered if I had taken him in a direction he did not wish to go. I just sat by quietly for several minutes. Almost as if he sensed I was going to conclude our visit, Stuart whispered, "I'm not afraid to die. I'm afraid of going to hell."

Since becoming an oncology chaplain, I have had more than one conversation with dying patients about where they believe they will spend eternity. Some patients are confident they will be in heaven, while some express concern about being unworthy. Stuart's voice trembled when he uttered those words, and I could not leave him there with his fear. My first thought was "Why?" but I knew that was strictly an information-seeking question. I leaned closer and asked Stuart if he wanted to say more about his fear of going to hell. As if it were not the cancer devouring him but the torture of a secret he carried, Stuart cried, "I killed a man!" Before I could gather my thoughts to respond, Stuart said, "God is going to send me straight to hell. I really need you to forgive me so God will forgive me." I was stunned!

He whispered, "I'm not afraid to die. I'm afraid of going to hell."

Somehow I managed to take a couple of minutes to consider how to handle this and prepare to continue our conversation. What followed was my offer to page a priest for Stuart to make his confession and receive the desired absolution. After Stuart's stern refusal of my offer, we engaged in a brief dialogue about confession. Stuart relentlessly clung to his need for *me*, as the chaplain he had confided in, to forgive him. For a minute or two, I felt we were having a circular conversation. I was not ordained at the time and knew I could not offer Stuart the pardon he so desperately sought. Stuart was undaunted by my argument. Finally, the light of divine intervention flickered on in my heart. This was absolutely not about me and what I could or could not do! I shifted the focus of forgiveness from me to Stuart.

With renewed compassion and a more confident voice, I lightly touched Stuart's trembling hand and spoke about the power of forgiveness burning in his heart. For Stuart's fear to dissolve into forgiveness, he had to be the one providing the pardon. I suggested that while Stuart was anxiously waiting for God to forgive him, God was waiting for Stuart to forgive himself. We talked of the pent-up hellish feelings that had tortured him for years after the crime and of the self-defensive nature of his act. Hesitant at first, Stuart eventually relaxed into releasing his self-contempt and began moving toward self-forgiveness.

Finally, we walked through a guided meditation that kept Stuart in the immediacy of the moment and connected with his feelings. With Stuart's fear melting, he thanked me for being there and helping him through a very difficult process. Even in the dimly lit room, I could see the tension drain from Stuart's eyes. I wondered if he needed some type of ritual to mark this momentous occasion. When I asked Stuart about that possibility, his bearded mouth seemed to curl into a tentative smile. Several ideas ensued, but the one he ultimately thought of and chose was "meeting God with a new heart and a clean face."

Almost enthusiastically, Stuart pushed the call button on his bed rail. A very surprised clinical assistant responded, "How can I help you?" In a clear voice, Stuart asked if someone could help him shave. After a few seconds of silence, the assistant assured Stuart that someone would come to his room. Stuart's puzzled nurse, Gabby, approached his bedside and was surprised to see me seated there. She explored his shaving request further, looked at me for consensus, and smiled as she told Stuart she would be delighted to shave him.

> *I placed the candle in Stuart's hands and listened as he recited the most meaningful prayer of self-forgiveness and love.*

Gabby became an instrumental part of this beautiful ritual. Preparing and shaving a very weak Stuart occurred in spurts, and she took her time with him. A fresh face emerged from beneath a mound of hair. Gabby found a mirror and held it for Stuart. I made a quick trip to my office to retrieve a battery-operated candle. When I returned, Stuart was still gazing into the mirror and smiling as tears rolled down both cheeks. Gabby found a pink breast cancer bandana and with Stuart's permission, tied it around his head, drawing his matted hair away from his face. He softly joked about whether or not God would recognize him when he got to heaven. I asked Stuart if he would like me to say a prayer for the occasion, and Gabby asked if she could participate. With Stuart's permission, we prayed together.

Afterward, Gabby politely left the room to give Stuart and me a moment together. I wondered aloud if Stuart wanted to offer his own prayer, and he nodded in agreement. I placed the candle in Stuart's hands and listened as he recited the most meaningful prayer of self-forgiveness and love I have ever heard. Although I cannot recall the precise words he uttered, I remember the heartfelt tenor of his voice. I knew Stuart meant every word.

Stuart and I said our good-byes through tears of joy and sorrow. Walking out the door, I knew he was in a more peaceful place. Stuart was hopeful for a few more days of life to enjoy his newfound tranquility. I was grateful for having been a witness to his life. I was especially thankful for the Holy Guidance that directed me toward Stuart's door earlier in the evening.

My telephone rang at six-thirty the next morning. Gabby was on the other end crying. She softly said, "Stuart's gone, Jo." By the time I arrived at the hospital, the team had bathed him in preparation for the arrival of funeral home staff. Gabby, Angela, and I took time to grieve, process, and ultimately rejoice in the healing power of presence, which transformed the final hours of Stuart's life.

Over the course of my own life I have become increasingly aware of how frequently I have not felt *heard*. Based on the sheer volume of available material on being present and listening to others, I am convinced I am not alone in my feelings. Thankfully, during my CPE residency, I came to realize that my sensitivity to being heard is a characteristic of strength rather than the weakness I once presumed it to be.

> *The letters in the words 'silent' and 'listen' are identical. Only the order is different. Each word contains the other.*

By "listening with the ears of our heart," as St. Benedict once said, we forge a space where suffering and hope can speak their healing words. When we engage in listening, we are truly present to another. But listening demands silence. The letters in the words *silent* and *listen* are identical. Only the order is different. Each word contains the other. Surely, that is no coincidence. For it seems we bestow humanity on each other when we pay attention to one another. Presence acts like a powerful soothing balm to heal psychic wounds. As chaplains—as human beings—may we always remember that being present graces others to discover their sacredness and initiates the spiritual process of healing.

Presence Prayer:

Ever-Present One,

Gently remind us of young Samuel's loving response as you summoned him. Samuel said, *"Speak, Lord, for your servant is listening."* How often we demand, "Listen, Lord, for your servant is speaking." *Speak to our hearts* so we hear you over the incessant noise of this fast-paced world. Please *slow our pace*, unplug us from the addictive temptations of technology, and *help us listen deeply to one another.*

May we gift each other with the blessing of true presence so our weary, *troubled souls* might *begin to heal*. As we become quiet, *may the world grow in stillness*. As we listen, may all ears be opened. As we heal, *may our world be renewed*. Amen.

Reflective Questions:

- When you consider someone you care about being your "witness," what thoughts or feelings arise?
- When was the last time you told your story?
- When was the last time you felt truly heard? Who listened?
- How do you respond physically, emotionally and spiritually when someone gives you their undivided attention?
- How do you respond when you feel as if you are not being heard? Center and quiet yourself to feel the pain of not being heard. Write a word or phrase about the feeling to remember the next time you have difficulty staying present with someone.
- What image(s) does the phrase "healing presence" evoke in you? Can you draw or describe the image(s)?
- How would you respond to Stuart's plea and his belief that he was going to hell?
- Consider spending ten minutes listening to the world around you. Separate each sound (wind, traffic, music, birds, etc.) and ponder the message of each.
- Whether or not you are a chaplain, how do you stay present with people you believe are detached, unengaged, or disinterested?

Blessed are the pure of heart, for they are reliably present.

Chapter Four

Be Compassionate

Compassion is hard because it requires the inner disposition to go with others to places where they are weak, vulnerable, lonely, and broken.
- Henri J.M. Nouwen

Four friends dropped by to console me.

Pity cried crocodile tears
as she walked past me,
plopping onto the overstuffed chair in the corner.
Through clumps of soggy tissue,
she soulfully mumbled how very, very sorry she was.
I offered her more tissues.

Sympathy was lost for words
and brought an expressive card to speak for her.
Lowering herself onto a straight-backed chair
with crossed legs, folded hands, and understanding eyes,
she gazed at me from across the room.
I smiled faintly at her.

Empathy offered an understanding hug,
feeling like it came from a place of experience.
She sat nearby, sharing her similar story
with an expression of knowingness
as a random tear rolled down her cheek.
I reached for her hand.

Compassion wrapped her arm around my shoulder,
walking in stride to the sofa
where we sat side-by-side.
In a kind voice as soft as a feather,
she simply said, "I'm here for you."
I felt my spirit sigh.

True compassion arises from a sense that the heart has the fearless capacity to embrace all things, to touch all things, to relate to all things.

- Jack Kornfield

Life had been difficult for Sara. Barely twenty-five years old, she had already given birth to three children. Just before her third child was born, the children's father made a decision. He vanished from their lives, leaving Sara as sole provider for her young family. Sara's mother and brother were unable to offer much in the way of assistance due to their own emotional and financial challenges. Thoughts of snow-free winters and greater employment opportunities enticed Sara to leave her familiar hometown in the Midwest. Hoping for a fresh start, Sara moved her three young children halfway across the country.

Within a short time of moving, Sara managed to find a job. Unfortunately, her new salary could not sustain a family of four. Day-care for seven-month-old Carrie and twenty-eight-month-old Connor put an enormous dent in her paycheck. Casey was five and starting kindergarten but required after-school care. Basic needs of shelter, food, child care, and clothing were financially overwhelming. It was then that Sara met Don, who appeared to be a god-send. Don's shift-work enabled him to help care for the children on most week days. For a few short months, his salary coupled with Sara's made life just a little easier for her and the children.

I first met Sara in the emergency room (ER). She was barefoot, wearing a soiled work uniform, and alternated between fingering unkempt blond hair around her ears and wiping her nose and tears with the cuff of her shirt. Sara appeared stunned. The atmosphere in the ER was frenzied, as it usually is when a tragedy occurs. My pager told the three-line story. So after a quick assessment of the immediate area and a brief introduction to Sara, I drew her away to a nearby private consultation room with the police following closely behind.

Sara's youngest child was dead. Although details of her death were still being gathered, ER medical staff and police were classifying Carrie's death as a "non-accidental trauma" (NAT). Carrie had been in Don's custody and initial evidence overwhelmingly pointed to him as the person who inflicted Carrie's fatal injuries. For a child—an infant in this case—to die at the hands of an adult is unconscionable. The tragedy shakes families, hospital staff, police, and medical examiners to the

For a child – an infant in this case – to die at the hands of an adult is unconscionable.

very core. Additionally, as humans, we often feel compelled to blame. Someone, usually the mother of the child, becomes a second victim. In the minds of emotional observers, a mother is expected to protect her children and is often held accountable for not doing a better job of mothering and protecting. From prior NAT-experiences, I knew that in the minds of many Sara had already been judged, tried, and convicted as culpable in Carrie's death.

Once the urgency of the moment dissipated, I would return to debrief the staff and give them a chance to process their feelings. At the height of the chaos, however, my most pressing ministry was to Sara. Apart from the unfolding details, Sara was Carrie's mother and had just been told her baby girl was dead. She was bewildered and grief-stricken. Hearing the news of Carrie's death was horrendous, and yet Sara also had to undergo intense questioning from police and Child Protective Services (CPS). My role through the process was to be a supportive presence for Sara. I did not have to question, judge, or validate her. That does not mean I was devoid of personal feelings about the tragedy. My stomach was turning, my heart pounding, and my mind racing with thoughts that would take me days, maybe weeks, to sort out. Training and experience had taught me to be aware of my internal responses to the situation while still being present to the needs of the patient. Sara was my patient, and she desperately needed a non-judgmental, compassionate chaplain by her side.

It was a horrible, terrible, disastrous day for everyone. For baby Carrie, who would not celebrate her first birthday, learn to swim, taste corn-on-the-cob, chase fireflies, or start school, the day meant the end of her all-too-young life. Don was taken to prison where he would await trial and if found guilty, most likely spend the remainder of his life. Sitting with Sara in the remnants of the day, I witnessed the brokenness of a young woman trying to comprehend that her infant daughter had been killed and that her boyfriend was deemed responsible. In addition, Sara's other two children, Casey and Conner, were removed from her custody. When the interrogations were over, Sara sat alone in a tiny consultation room with no one but a stranger she kept calling "Chaplain." Initially, I was there because it was my turn to carry the trauma pager; however, I stayed with Sara in spite of my conflicted feelings because I believe deeply in a theology of compassion.

When the interrogations were over, Sara sat alone in a tiny consultation room with no one but a stranger she kept calling "Chaplain."

What does it mean to have a theology of compassion? A wise teacher once instructed me to break down anything that seems overwhelming into manageable tasks or smaller pieces. As a student, I learned the origin of the word theology and understood it to mean the study of

God's nature and God's relation to the universe. Typically, dictionaries define theology as a study of religious faith, practice, and experience. Without a doubt, the definition I read and discussed in my first theology class years ago stays with me as the simplest and most meaningful: "Faith seeking understanding." Saint Anselm of Canterbury, the remarkable eleventh century Christian philosopher, is credited with these profound words of wisdom, which continue to resonate with theology students of all ages. For me, definitions usually serve the purpose of shining a narrow beam of light to assist my comprehension of a word or phrase. However, when I first read St. Anselm's definition, I felt as though a giant door had flung open, revealing a limitless universe of possibility and granting me permission to be curious about everything, including God.

I felt as though a giant door had flung open giving me permission to be curious about everything, including God.

One of the countless curiosities theology awakened in me is the power of words. I frequently notice words within words. For example, as I write about being *called*, I notice the words *all* and *led* within. The word *prepared* contains *pared,* meaning to peel back or trim an outer layer. Changing the order of a few letters reveals other words that for me are related to being prepared: *read, prep, reap,* and of course, *dare*.

In considering the word *compassion,* I am inspired by its origin from two Latin words meaning to bear or suffer (pati) with (com-). Looking further, inside the word *compassion* I also see *compass.* Interestingly, the compass is a magnetic instrument which helps us find our way or direction. Another type of compass most of us used in school allowed us to steady the point of the instrument and gently twirl the penciled end to form a perfect circle. All of these concepts form an image of chaplains as instruments encircling the vulnerable with supportive loving-kindness that sustains sufferers until they regain directional perspective.

In its purest form, a theology of compassion restates an ancient axiom common to every religion in the world and typically summarized as the *Golden Rule*: Do unto others as you would have them do unto you. Christian scriptures are peppered with teachings on this topic. In the Gospel of Matthew, we find, "So in everything, do to others as you would have them do to you; this sums up the law and the prophets" (Matt 7:12). Luke's Gospel echoes, "Do to others as you would have them do to you" (Luke 6:31). How we treat each other is foundational to our existence, evidenced by how often countless prophetic teachers remind us of the significance of loving others—even our enemies. From

> *A theology of compassion can be summarized as the Golden Rule: Do unto others as you would have them do unto you.*

Buddhism to Zoroastrianism, holy texts call upon us to love and care for one another in an ethic of reciprocity: Treat others the way you would like to be treated. The current Dalai Lama articulates this beautifully by saying, "My religion is kindness."

The Golden Rule is a fundamental and simple principle for living and yet one of the most difficult to apply. Like the concept of faith, the need to offer compassion generally surfaces in situations of trial and suffering. While professing to hold a theology of compassion is as easy as saying or typing the words, living it out entails wading into the messiness of life. When we treat others as we hope to be treated, we grow roots on our tree of life. When I treat patients, families, and staff with compassion, my theology of compassion deepens. I am putting a religion of kindness into action, despite any conflicting feelings. I am able to meet people where they are, instead of expecting or coercing them to respond, behave or believe according to my standards. I think of this as a conviction of the heart.

How did my theology of compassion comfort Sara in the midst of her agony? What about the hospital staff, police, and Child Protective Services personnel? How did my theology of compassion help me in the hours and days following the incident? With slings and arrows of spoken and unspoken blame flying around the emergency room, I can honestly say it was not easy. Standing in the gap as a non-anxious presence, I tried to step into each person's suffering in a transformative way. To do so meant setting aside all attachments I had to particular outcomes. Again, not easy.

Having no attachment to outcomes is not the same as denying personal feelings. I felt enraged that an adult would inflict injury on a child and cause her death. I felt immense sorrow for Carrie, whose life had been snuffed out before she learned to walk, and for her siblings, who lost a sister and mother on the same day. I felt angry about a world where a young mother is so financially desperate. I felt judgmental about the nurses and police who were condemning Sara. Days later, those feelings fueled personal reflection on judging the judgers. However, despite these overwhelming and conflicting feelings, I managed to encourage Sara to take a few deep breaths with me, and as a result, we both grew calmer. Listening to Sara share her life story, I noticed the hard edges of my conflicted feelings begin to soften. Empathy made me receptive to hearing Sara's story, but compassion called me to respond to her plight and gave me courage to help birth layers of story etched in her memory. As she talked, I found myself wondering how this young woman would carry on with her life. Who would be

> *Empathy made me receptive to hearing her story, but compassion called me to respond and gave me courage to help birth layers of stories etched in her memory.*

with her as she grieved? Was Sara capable of climbing out of her deep well of guilt? She was so alone.

While empathy tends to stir up a response to another's *feelings*, compassion stimulates a response to the *situation*. Compassion in action involves a team of people. The social worker and I made numerous telephone calls seeking assistance for Sara. Police Victim Services came to assist and ultimately drove her home. Grief counseling connections were made, and the few people Sara referred to as "sorta friends" were called to be with her that evening. Walking Sara to the car, I could not fathom what her life would be like in the foreseeable future. I imagined her standing alone at the graveside of her baby, an image of Sara that still haunts me. It may be the terrible way Carrie died, or it may be that Sara symbolizes all grieving mothers whose children die at the hands of abusers. More likely it is a combination of factors. Despite the healing power of counseling and time, neither the victims nor those of us who minister to them ever *get over* a loss or completely move on. Losses like this become part of who we are.

After Sara left the emergency room, I realized my ministry concerning this heartbreaking event was not over. Staff also needed my time, attention, and compassion. Once again, I became aware of my conflicted feelings and prayed for compassion to guide me in a quest for neutrality. Nurses and physicians showed a wide range of reactions with anger and helplessness by far the most predominate. There was no way to resuscitate and save Carrie. For medical staff, being unable to save a life is irreconcilable and devastating. Non-accidental traumas are excruciating from every perspective. When they result in death, staff members grieve along with everyone else. A process debriefing session gives staff an opportunity to express their thoughts and feelings in a safe environment, without fear of judgment or reprisal. Chaplains play a key role in this effective model of care, often as both initiator and facilitator. Although debriefings are kept to an hour, staff support from chaplains is an on-going process. It is not uncommon for many staff to seek counsel privately about the event months afterwards. Each conversation has the potential to aid the healing process.

> *A child's death is so unimaginable, so unspeakable there is no word to define those left behind.*

Whenever a child dies, the emotional toll is palpable. Whether from disease, accident, violence, or illness, the death of a child is always tragic and never natural. The English language provides words to describe spouses and children after the death of their loved ones. We use words like widow, widower, and orphan to invoke meaning for the loss. However, there is no fitting word to adequately describe those left behind after the loss of a child. In life and in death, parents are always parents; and yet, they struggle with response to a simple question: How many children do you have? In the event of a child's death, perhaps the only meaningful word and response is compassion—for everyone affected.

Long after Carrie's death, feelings of compassion for her mother lingered. Sara had also been a victim of the crime that killed her daughter. Eventually, she was put in contact with the National Organization of Parents of Murdered Children (POMC), with whom she maintains an active relationship. After years of extremely painful emotional and spiritual work, Sara is becoming her own compass, making a path through her grief, developing healthy coping skills, and starting to live again.

During a follow-up telephone call weeks after the tragedy, Sara gave me a precious, unexpected gift. She told me that on the day she "fell into hell," I had been "Jesus with skin on" for her. I will never forget her voice or the sound of compassion echoing in my ear. Sometimes when I take a few deep breaths to center myself as I walk to the next difficult encounter, or for no particular reason at all, Sara comes to mind. I pray she knows that I am breathing with her, just as we did together on that fateful day.

Compassion Prayer:

God of Comfort,

The warmth of *Divine consolation* provides comfort when I am afflicted and *permeates* every step of *my human journey*. May *I* strive to embody you as I *accept your invitations* to weep with those who weep, *to comfort* those in need of comforting, *and* to wade into and *bear witness to* the pain and *suffering* of others *without judgment*.

Your children are hurting. *Compassion is messy*. Compassion is *not easy*. Compassion *begs for action*. I will follow. *Show me the way.*

Amen.

Reflective Questions:

- What color is compassion for you?
- Can you think of a time in your life when someone unexpectedly showed you compassion? What was the impact of that experience?
- Has there ever been a time when you declined offering compassion to someone in need? Was it someone you knew or a stranger? How did that experience affect you?
- What does the *Golden Rule* mean to you? How do you practice it in daily life and in your ministry?
- As you contemplate having a personal theology, what images or words come to mind? Draw the images or write down the words.
- What is it about compassion that stretches or challenges you?
- Who/Where/ What is God for you in the messiness of life?
- If you are currently a chaplain, when did you last find yourself in the throes of a situation calling for a compassionate approach to varying beliefs, and how did you handle your own feelings?

Blessed are the compassionate, for they are the comforters.

Chapter Five

Be Accountable

I always wondered why somebody doesn't do something about that. Then I realized I was somebody.

- Lily Tomlin

What is ***accountability***

if not a choice between

tucking your head into

a safe sweet spot of comfort

and sticking your neck out for

a heartfelt fervent conviction?

Is the answer found in heartbeats

safely slowing down

to a sustainable, easy pace or

speeding up in risk

with lavishly renewing oxygen

for the meaning of life?

You may never know what results come of your action, but if you do nothing, there will be no result.
- Mahatma Gandhi

Dr. Seuss authored countless books, providing children and adults with hours of rhyming entertainment. As a young mother reading Seuss to my daughter, I noticed deeper philosophical themes running throughout the longer stories and used them as teaching moments. *Horton Hears a Who* remains one of my favorites. In the jungle environment of Nool, Horton encounters an entire community of microscopic beings living on a single clover leaf. Although he is an elephant, Horton sticks his neck out like a turtle to engage the mayor of Whoville in conversation about the plight of the Whos. From that point forward, Horton decides to dedicate his life to protecting the Whos in Whoville from the dangers of the much larger world. Of course, no one but Horton is able to see or hear the Whos. But that does not stop Horton from defending the tiny critters of Whoville. The concept of the largest animal, an elephant, hearing and advocating for the tiniest of critters, a Who, brings a smile to my face.

Horton understands what it means to speak up for the vulnerable. He holds himself accountable for those whose size, influence, or voice is too small to be heard. One of the most famous quotes from the story is Horton announcing, "A person's a person no matter how small." Horton also knows that accountability and advocacy require taking risks. For him, the risks center on disbelief and ridicule; however, the gains outweigh any potential negative consequences. By the end of the story, Horton, with help from the mayor and a young boy named Jojo, saves the entire community of Whos from destruction and thus personifies my metaphor for accountability and advocacy. Horton, the mayor, and Jojo each made a choice between safely ignoring the situation by tucking their heads in and steadfastly advocating for the Whos in Whoville by sticking their necks out.

Horton understands what it means to speak up for the vulnerable. He knows that being an advocate requires taking risks.

While the words may not be completely interchangeable, I think accountability and advocacy are very similar when used to define one of the main functions of board-certified chaplains. Generally, accountability means taking responsibility for an act or behavior. Advocacy is speaking or pleading on behalf of someone. Spiritual care professionals are trained patient advocates and as such, are expected to take certain risks in standing up for their patients' rights and well-being.

Being accountable to and functioning as an advocate for patients can take many forms. Here is just one example: Not long ago, I opened my work email to find a note from a woman I had met several years ago when her young son, Hunter, was hospitalized. Jennifer and I had exchanged emails only once after Hunter was discharged. Now, without giving a reason, Jennifer wanted to know if I would meet her for lunch. Interestingly, three days before receiving Jennifer's email, I had been reviewing my journal notes and considered incorporating Hunter's story into this chapter on accountability and advocacy. The overlapping of these events caused me to reflect further on what it means to stick my neck out and to speak up for the vulnerable. It also confirmed my decision to include his story.

The day I met Hunter and Jennifer, I was driving to work, quietly reflecting in preparation for whatever the day might hold. On this particular morning, as I drove the short distance from home to hospital, my pager suddenly began beeping. Before I could safely reach for it, my cell phone rang. I knew something unusual was unfolding. At a traffic light, I reached for the pager and glanced at the message. The digits were familiar. I quickly recognized them as the extension for my primary unit of coverage. As soon as possible, I telephoned the staff and was promptly asked by the charge nurse, "Where are you? How quickly can you get here? We have a situation and we need your help."

In less than ten minutes I was standing at the nurses' station being filled in by the team leader. I listened as she informed me about a new problem that had developed for five-year-old Hunter, who was recently diagnosed with juvenile diabetes. He and his mother were still reeling from the diagnosis and all the changes it meant for their lives. At five years of age, Hunter would begin the routine of pricking his finger, testing his blood sugar level, receiving insulin injections, and managing his food choices. Hunter and his mother, Jennifer, had received extensive education about all this just the day before. According to the medical team, Hunter was an adorable and bright five-year-old, but like anyone diagnosed with diabetes, he was definitely unhappy about the "sticks." As serious as this situation was for Hunter and his mother, I had a strong sense that there was something else disturbing everyone.

At five years of age, Hunter would begin the routine of pricking his finger, testing his blood sugar level, receiving insulin injections, and managing his food choices.

Looking around, I noticed the gathering at the nurses' station included several other nurses from the day and prior night shifts. With each one adding a statement of explanation, I recognized tension in their posture and irritation in their voices. Apparently, a small group of well-intentioned members of a local church had dropped by the hospital the evening before. They had moved through the facility until locating a unit where the entry doors were open and a friendly staff member was willing to speak with them. After inquiring about patients or families who might want someone to pray with them, the church members were directed to one family. While this first family was pleased to have prayers offered, what happened next created a huge dilemma for Jennifer and her son.

Having a child hospitalized for any reason is especially stressful, so what often happens is that patients and families sometimes become acquainted with one another, especially when hospital stays extend beyond a day. In this situation, the initial family prayed for by the church threesome was aware of Hunter's new diagnosis. Meaning no harm, they suggested that the group go to his room and offer prayers. I was beginning to get the picture. I was on a damage-control mission. Not just for Hunter and his mother but also for the unit staff.

Life has taught me that multiple eyewitness accounts of an event often result in many variations concerning the details. Each individual's perspective is affected by personal life experiences and culture. Because a pediatric environment is fertile ground for nurturing protective attitudes toward patients, it is imperative for chaplains to maintain the delicate balance between neutrality and support for staff concerns. Although I often receive updates from staff regarding referrals, my goal is to enter a patient's room as a blank slate. In doing so, the patient and family are given an opportunity to relate their personal points of view regarding the experience, without fear of my possible preconceived notions or ideas. This is one way of honoring the patient's narrative.

It is imperative for chaplains to maintain the delicate balance between neutrality and support for staff concerns.

In this instance, most staff members were angry because, in their eyes, uninvited guests came onto their unit and caused a young patient considerable distress. Thinking they could have prevented the situation, others felt guilty they had not been present on the unit at the time, or if there, did not notice the threesome arrive. Each person expressed concern about the vulnerability of pediatric patients and the staff's inability to protect Hunter.

The well-intentioned threesome had entered Hunter's room, introduced themselves, and after a brief conversation with Jennifer and Hunter, asked if they could pray for him. Jennifer and I had not met prior to this incident, so she mistakenly thought this group was sanctioned by the hospital to provide pastoral care. As a spiritual person, Jennifer also presumed that prayer might benefit her son, who was really struggling with the impact of his new diagnosis. According to Jennifer, the small group gathered around Hunter and prayed about how God does not want children to have diabetes. Jennifer recalled thinking that was probably a very true statement. But then the three visitors continued their prayer by addressing how God would take Hunter's diabetes away if he would just pray hard enough and believe strongly enough for it to happen. Jennifer was shocked and unable to speak for a minute or two while the group continued to stress how Hunter just needed to trust that God would take his diabetes away.

> *But then the three visitors suggested God would take Hunter's diabetes away if he prayed hard enough and believed it was true.*

Jennifer shared how rapidly thoughts, such as why she granted the threesome access to Hunter's room and how she was going to get them out, crossed her mind. Jennifer could not imagine the hospital approving of this distorted prayer activity, and she also knew that serious damage had just occurred and would not be easily undone. As soon as the group left, Hunter inquired why his mother had asked them to leave and why she didn't want God to take his diabetes away. Jennifer felt she was in an untenable position with her son. She believed in God and prayer. She had also raised her children to pray. However, she was very concerned about Hunter's new attitude toward diabetes, not to mention his confusion about her own behavior.

Concrete thinking is part and parcel to the

developmental stage of a five-year-old. Abstract concepts are far too complex for very young children to grasp. Hunter completely understood the reality of being stuck with needles and was delighted to be introduced to anything that would make those needles unnecessary. The prayerful strangers who had come into his room had given Hunter a reason to decline both the testing pricks and insulin injections. As Jennifer reported, "He is one happy camper right now."

Responses to such a tragic event are often based upon each individual's area of expertise. Nurse educators teach patients and families about the disease and treatment plan so they can care for themselves after discharge from the hospital. Child life specialists also work closely with pediatric patients. Trained in child development, they expertly assist patients in understanding what is being done to and for them medically. As a chaplain, I have strong feelings about my role as patient advocate. I feel a responsibility to protect the emotional and spiritual vulnerability of patients and their families during hospitalizations.

> *Jennifer was very concerned about Hunter's new attitude toward diabetes and his confusion about her own behavior.*

The church group who entered the hospital likely had good intentions. They believed that suffering patients and families might benefit from their presence and prayers, which include that if someone prays and believes enough, God will take away a disease. They also truly believe evangelizing and saving souls is their calling from God. The person who admitted the prayerful threesome to the unit was a woman of faith who knew one family on the unit well enough to trust they would appreciate extra prayers. That particular family had learned about Hunter's new diagnosis and felt he and his mother might also benefit from prayer. A domino effect had occurred.

Our young patient, Hunter, desperately wanted both diabetes and needles to be part of a bad dream from which he would awaken. He wanted his pre-diabetes life back and was very receptive to praying for God to hear and answer the church group's prayer. Hunter's mother found herself caught between supporting her son's desire to be diabetes-free and the medical evidence proving he was not. Every time the staff tried to test Hunter's blood sugar, tears flowed as he begged his mother not to let them stick him. When he required insulin, more tears ran down his cheeks. Hunter insisted his mother "pray more" so God would take his diabetes away. Jennifer was distraught that strangers who had come into the room were now causing her son so much spiritual, emotional, and physical distress.

Although he is an intelligent child, Hunter's age and circumstances made him especially susceptible to the type of situation that occurred in his room. Jennifer is a bright, articulate, spiritual woman and devoted mother who was caught off-guard by the intrusion. Almost immediately after the threesome left Hunter's room, Jennifer telephoned her former pastor to ventilate her feelings and to seek counsel on how to proceed with her son. With his help, they got through the evening; however, by the next morning, emotions were erupting again. The dawn of a new day meant more glucose testing and further insulin injections for a wounded warrior named Hunter.

> *Jennifer was distraught that strangers who had come into the room were now causing her son so much spiritual, emotional, and physical distress.*

Everyone, including Hunter, was back to square one on the issue of diabetes. The nurse educator was called back to re-teach Hunter. The child life specialist was brought back to assist. I was there to help Hunter explore his theology of prayer, miracles, and God as healer. Unfortunately, the backdrop had changed. Hunter was now armed with a stronger resistance shaped by a five-year-old's desperate need to be free of diabetes and a new reason to believe it was possible.

Sitting next to Hunter, I alternated between gently exploring what God meant to him and giving him space to express grief about his new diagnosis. With childlike confidence, Hunter beautifully articulated his sense of God as "love," immediately followed by restating what the church visitors had told him about God not wanting children to have diabetes. A five-year-old can only tolerate so much exploration of thought and feeling. We were at an impasse, and I knew Hunter needed a break from further discussion. With that in mind, I turned to his mother.

Jennifer was guilt-ridden for having permitted the prayer group into Hunter's room. Chaplains understand that telling someone not to feel the way they do is not only ineffective but also dismissive. Rather than assuring Jennifer she had no way of knowing what the church team would say, I invited her to talk about what had happened the night before. After her thorough reflection and dialogue of the entire episode, Jennifer looked at me and said, "I guess I really could not have predicted what they would say or do, huh?" I smiled at her in agreement. Then we talked about how to help her son in the days ahead. Hunter was given a cloth doll "who also had diabetes." After being encouraged to tell a story about his "diabetes doll," Hunter managed to project some of his own feelings into the story and onto the doll. He was even allowed to use un-needled syringes to give his doll friend insulin.

> *Chaplains understand that telling someone not to feel the way they do is not only ineffective but also dismissive.*

After several hours, Hunter became somewhat less tearful about all that had happened to him over the span of a few days. Of course, he was discharged as soon as medically ready. I wish I could report that Hunter left the hospital feeling better about his diabetes, but according to his mother, months passed before this happened.

The ongoing work of patient advocacy continued after Hunter was discharged from the hospital. Equipped with the knowledge of what happened to him and a new concern that something similar could happen again, I felt compelled to take action on more than one front. The next morning, during a structured daily briefing with approximately sixty leadership staff, I reported the incident. Immediately following the meeting, I was surrounded by physicians and nurses inquiring about how the child was doing and encouraging me to work with security on developing a tighter visitation policy.

We organized a team of leaders from several appropriate fields: security, child life, patient representatives, clinical managers, chaplaincy, volunteer services, and patient-centered care. The charge of the newly-founded committee was to research and discuss ideas for protecting vulnerable patients. The challenge was how to maintain the fragile balance of reasonably free access to patients by family members and friends in the process. Whatever plan we collectively decided upon also needed to pass the budget test. Recommending an expensive overhaul to the existing badge-entry system would not pass an economic preview; therefore, extensive research about options was needed.

Accessibility is one of the environmental characteristics of patient-centered care. Creating balance between patient access and security is often a challenge in hospitals, particularly pediatric hospitals. Young children respond better when family is nearby. Nurses benefit when parents are involved in creating a setting of comfort and care around very young patients. In this case, the advocacy group believed it was important to learn what policies and procedures other hospitals around the country had implemented. What we learned was not surprising. Although no other hospital had incurred a similar incident, most hospitals with pediatric units required visitors to wear special identifying badges or arm bracelets. In some places, family members had a code name to remember. Pediatric unit doors were kept closed, with access granted only when the visitors pressed a button, stated the room number, and gave the code name. On critical care units, we had identical procedures. At a future meeting, the advocacy group presented their findings.

> *The charge of the newly-founded committee was to research and discuss ideas for protecting our vulnerable patients.*

In addition, after interviewing staff and working with security, I was able to determine which local church had sanctioned the visitors. Several telephone conversations with the pastor afforded me opportunities to address the extreme vulnerability of young patients and their families. I also shared the damaging outcome of one patient's experience and the extensive staff involvement needed to help the child recover from it and move forward.

Visitors wishing to have access to patients for a specific purpose are viewed as volunteers. As such, they are required to be screened and trained through volunteer services. Ultimately, we recommended that all interested church members communicate through a spokesperson with the director of volunteer services. After a screening interview, training, and required immunizations were up-to-date, volunteers would be better prepared to visit patients. Training of hospital volunteers is wide-ranging. Candidates are extensively briefed on the Health Insurance Portability and Accountability Act (HIPAA) regulations pertaining to patient confidentiality. They learn about organizational policies and procedures surrounding matters such as dress code, proselytizing, and workplace violence. Volunteerism requires dedication and commitment.

In the end, a few modifications to hospital visitation procedures were implemented, with minimal impact to legitimate patient access. During a conversation between the director of volunteers and the prayer group's representative, various methods were discussed by which members of her group could become trained volunteers.

In a follow-up conversation after Hunter's discharge,

Jennifer was informed about the formation of an advocacy team and its efforts toward tighter security. She had been impressed with the ways the staff rallied to support her son at a time of emotional and spiritual distress. She expressed her appreciation and also remarked about how struck she had been by our conversation on spirituality in Hunter's room. Little did I know that a potentially life-changing seed had been planted in Jennifer's spirit that day.

I was quite surprised when, years later, I received an email from Jennifer. During our lunch meeting, the focus of discussion was not Hunter, but career paths. Even more surprising was Jennifer's revelation about her burgeoning interest in healthcare ministry. She was particularly curious about hospital chaplaincy. Her enthusiasm for ministry was palpable. Listening to Jennifer's questions reminded me of when I turned toward my own tugging call to chaplaincy. I am now honored to accompany Jennifer as she explores the possibility of a new call on her life.

> *Little did I know that a potentially life-changing seed had been planted in Jennifer's spirit that day.*

We concluded our first lunch meeting with an update on Jennifer's family. Hunter still has juvenile diabetes, but he views it differently after all these years. The change in her son was most certainly not immediate. Jennifer and her husband patiently and persistently helped Hunter understand

and accept his diabetes. He received appropriate counseling and had a wonderful experience attending a camp for children with diabetes.

While the fictional Whos in Whoville had one primary advocate in Horton, there had been numerous "Hortons" rallying for young Hunter. I was honored and grateful to be one of them. Each person touched by the experience became an advocate for the little guy whose voice was not strong enough to be heard. One of the rewards came when Jennifer shared that an older, wiser Hunter came to believe that "diabetes makes him special."

Eventually, Jennifer will decide whether or not to return to school and pursue healthcare ministry as a chaplain. She was encouraged by our conversations and the fact that I was older than she is now when I changed careers. Jennifer was also surprised to hear that my decision to become a chaplain stemmed from a tragic event in my own life. We have shared other stories of how frequently good results flow out from a disaster. Furthermore, I am deeply and profoundly touched by the unique *power of presence* chaplains offer during pastoral visits. The demeanor of a chaplain during a crisis can have far-reaching effects. Time and relationships may help water the seeds we plant. In this particular case, I was privileged to

> *The demeanor of a chaplain during a crisis can have far-reaching effects.*

learn that my intervention during Hunter's crisis was a catalyst for Jennifer's heart stirrings toward chaplaincy.

Accountability Prayer:

Gracious Advocate

As the universe unfolds, *opportunities abound* for me to stand up and *to speak out* on behalf of the voiceless. Like a turtle longing for the comfort of a safe shell, *I tend to hide* from all that scares me. *Hesitation and fear* too often *keep me* ineffective and *paralyzed*. I miss the chance to reach out and help someone in need.

Living in community, *I have a responsibility* for the well-being of others. *Grace me* with courage to make a difference in big and small ways. *When* I am faced with decisions and *I am tempted to pull back*, support my efforts *to move toward* life-giving choices. May I risk what I think is a shelter from the storm for *the firmness of my convictions*. Amen.

Reflective Questions:

- What would you have said to comfort Hunter? How would you have tried to help Jennifer with her own guilt and sadness? How would you have helped the staff?
- How do you as a chaplain attempt to help patients and their families who have been hurt understand that sometimes even those who wish to offer spiritual solace can do harm? How do you make peace with this in your own heart?
- What is the most intense value or belief you hold, and what would you do to protect or defend it?
- When, if ever, have you felt like a turtle tucking in your head for safety? Recall a time when you stuck your neck out for a cause. Which felt better: When you chose an easier path or when you spoke up for yourself or someone else? Why?
- If it is difficult for you to take a stand, reflect on ways for you to find your own voice.

Blessed are the advocates,

for they speak for the voiceless.

Chapter Six

Be Mindful

Maturity is that time when the mirrors in our mind turn to windows, and instead of seeing the reflection of ourselves, we see others.
-- Unknown

The impossibility of it,
walking past an open window without stopping
to notice what it offers,
each an invitation, a threshold, if you will.
Like a moth to a flame
I'm drawn to open windows,
be it for slanted light streaming into the room
or the stealthy silence of foggy night air,
mockingbirds chuckling at my inability to fly
or moonlight casting shadows on the sleepy earth below,
migrating monarchs dancing their way south on crisp fall breezes
or distant droning sirens of rescue urging me to prayer.

Do these fragile *boundaries* of glass
summon the world in
or seal it out?
Do steely metal locks
protect me from the world's cruelty
or insulate me from experiencing
life's heart-breaking sorrows and sacred, sweet joys?
Whom and to what do I grant entrance
or persist in keeping out?
Something always draws me to an open window.
Life...
an open window on the world and into my soul,
I choose
to close,
to lock,
or fling wide open.

Between stimulus and response there is a space. In that space is our power to choose our response. In our response lies our growth and our freedom.
- Viktor E. Frankl

From the time we are about two years of age, we have begun the process of pushing and testing boundaries. Even before developing the verbal skills to plead their cases, toddlers express their instinctive desire for independence through emotional outbursts. Most of us have witnessed these little ones in grocery or department stores when they are prevented from having something they want. Usually, we can hear these toddlers before we see them because they are crying or screaming, which is no doubt causing considerable embarrassment to the accompanying parent. Some of us label these toddlers as strong-willed, while others describe them as testing their boundaries in an age-appropriate manner.

Reaching back in my memory bank, I recall a favorite independence-seeking toddler story from a dear friend with twin boys. One day, with Andy sitting on her lap, Holly was attempting to put on and tie his shoes. Andy kept kicking and shouting, "I can do it, I can do it," while his mother struggled to simply get the task done and move on to the copious other challenges involved in raising toddler twin boys. Holly repeatedly and unsuccessfully explained to Andy that he did not know how to tie his shoes yet and that she was going to do it for him until he was skilled enough to learn. As his brother, David, stood close by observing the situation, Andy continued pleading his case, with each insistence growing louder. Exasperated, Holly, who prides herself in not talking down to her children, asserted, "Andy, I've been on this planet longer than you have and I am going to tie your shoes." With that, Andy immediately ceased squirming, raised his head up to look his mother in the face, and said with the total wide-eyed awe of a two-year-old, "*You've* been on a *planet*?" Holly told me she laughed so hard that even *she* had a difficult time getting Andy's shoes tied. As she later recounted, "Who would have thought the word *planet* could stop a two-year-old in his tracks long enough to get his shoes tied?"

Although sometimes diversion is an effective boundary technique, toddlers grow up to become teens and then adults. Diversion as a method for establishing boundaries loses its effectiveness as we mature. We tend to believe we know what's best, and we often prefer unrestricted freedom. On the other hand, becoming familiar with written regulations can save lives. And learning about cultural boundaries can save embarrassment.

Reflecting on my journey from volunteer chaplain to board-certified chaplain, I am humbled and grateful for the countless lessons patients, families, and staff have taught me about cultural sensitivity and boundaries. Being culturally sensitive is a particularly significant component of chaplaincy. It is important to note that culture consists of the values, beliefs, feelings, and behaviors characterizing an entire society or specific groups within society. Cultural sensitivity involves being informed and aware of the differences in those attitudes *without assigning values* to them, such as good, bad, better, worse, right, or wrong. While earning a Master's Degree in Theology helped prepare me for a culturally sensitive ministry, my daily pastoral encounters with diverse humanity are unsurpassed as the true teachable moments of my life. And, more often than not, these remarkable moments of learning come when I am in a position that challenges a personal boundary or value.

Being culturally sensitive is a particularly significant component of chaplaincy.

During my time as a hospice volunteer, I met Jeff. Although the friendship with and subsequent death of my dear friend Judy propelled me toward chaplaincy, my encounter with Jeff was a pivotal experience on the journey. In retrospect, I have often wondered if it was a *butterfly moment* sent from Judy, especially since I was oblivious to the impact of the experience until several days later.

Late one evening when the telephone calls and visitors at the hospice center had waned, I aimlessly wandered the halls. Initially, my roaming began as a means to stretch my legs, with no other agenda in mind. Most of the patients were alone and either unresponsive or asleep by this time. Dimmed lights in the hallways and rooms created a tranquil environment. This particular evening, however, I noticed a brighter light shining from inside one of the rooms. Stepping quietly through the doorway, I saw a young man with sunken eyes turning his head to look at me. My eyebrows went up in surprise, more due to his wakefulness than his appearance. Accustomed to the dim light, he noticed my facial response. He paused as if waiting to see if I would turn to leave. Instead, I stood by silently for several minutes. I really had no idea what to say or do. I was a volunteer who answered telephones and permitted visitors entrance to the building.

> *In retrospect, I have wondered if meeting Jeff was a butterfly moment sent from Judy.*

Finally, I nervously and apologetically introduced myself as "one of the volunteers." He said nothing, and I grew more anxious. Then, I took a timid step toward his bed and inquired, "What's *your* name?" Again, no response from him generated an increased level of anxiety in me. Feeling as though I had intruded into a private space, I offered my apology for bothering him and slowly turned back toward the door. Before I could take a step, I heard him say, “Why?” I looked over my shoulder and curiously asked, “Why did I bother you?” “No,” he whispered, “why are you a volunteer?” I smiled inwardly and turned to face him again, this time with more confidence. I told him my reason for volunteering was a long story, and he replied by telling me he “had no plans for the rest of the evening.” With that, we both grinned, and what followed was Jeff introducing himself and inviting me to stay awhile. I took a seat in the overstuffed chair a few feet from Jeff’s bed and let him know that I would tell him about my volunteer story right after he shared his story.

As if testing my mettle, Jeff began by telling me he was thirty-four years old and dying from AIDS. In those days, being diagnosed with HIV while living in a conservative corner of the Bible Belt could only mean two things: rejection and isolation. My initial response was, “I am truly sad that you are dying, Jeff, and I’m also curious about who you are besides a very young man with AIDS?” Seemingly pleased that AIDS was not my focal point, Jeff relaxed into his story. One of the things he shared that resonated with me was that he was Buddhist—also uncommon in that area. I recall exploring with him how he came to choose that spiritual path and what being a Buddhist meant to him.

During that evening, I learned many things about Buddhism, and even more about Jeff. What happened in the closing moments of our time together lingers in my memory. When I noticed Jeff growing tired, I suggested we conclude our conversation and pick it up again the next week when I would be returning to volunteer. With a wistful look in his eyes, Jeff shared that it was unlikely he would still be alive next week. Before I could reply, he simply said, "Would you pray for me?" Stumbling for a response, I finally blurted out, "I don't know how to pray for a Buddhist." Jeff grinned politely and gently encouraged me to pray the way I would for anyone else. Jeff's gentleness inspired my response, but I think it was more than that. I believe that *Someone Greater* spoke through me that evening when I looked at Jeff and said, "What if I pray for you in my tradition, and then you pray for both of us in your tradition?"

> *He simply said, "Would you say a prayer for me?" Stumbling for a response, I blurted out, "I don't know how to pray for a Buddhist."*

Jeff nodded and asked me to help him sit up in the bed. I was amazed that he had the strength, but with the head of the bed powered to its uppermost position, Jeff managed to sit quite straight. Resting his hands in his lap, Jeff held his fingers and thumbs together in the form of an "O" and even attempted to cross his legs. Sitting back down on the overstuffed chair with feet flat on the floor and eyes closed, I uttered a prayer for Jeff's journey from this world. I concluded my prayer by asking the Spirit of God to enfold Jeff in a special way so that Jeff would know from this day forward that he was never alone. When I finished, Jeff began his prayer, which was a lovely Buddhist chant. Although I did not understand any of the words, the tone was overwhelmingly gentle and moving. When Jeff was done chanting, I opened my eyes and saw a young man with tears rolling down his face. I presumed the tears were about his impending death. I was only partly correct. My curious look prompted a whispered statement from Jeff that I will never forget. Through his tears and with a trembling voice, Jeff said, “No one has ever asked me to pray in my tradition before. You can’t imagine what that means to me.” And he was right. I could not envision the impact of my simple invitation, but I will always remember Jeff’s endearing response.

When I returned the following week, his nurse, Carolyn, tearfully told me that Jeff had died peacefully in his sleep two nights after our praying together. She thanked me for “what I had done for Jeff in his last days.” Jeff had informed his nurse about our prayers. Nurse Carolyn let me know that even though no one was in Jeff’s room at the time of his death, Jeff had told her that after my prayer he felt

Nurse Carolyn tearfully told me that Jeff had died peacefully in his sleep two nights after our praying together.

"bathed in a comforting Presence." Once again, the blessings were reciprocal. I remember Jeff's words every time I encounter diverse cultural and religious backgrounds. I remain mindful of all I have yet to learn. Jeff is still speaking to me. He was and continues to be instrumental in shaping my cultural sensitivity as a chaplain.

However, as the quote from Viktor Frankl at the beginning of this chapter suggests to me, a placeholder for growth is found in the space between stimulus and response. Not every interaction with patients has ended as satisfactorily for me or for my patients. Kathy's memory lingers with me also, but for a very different reason. Kathy was a woman in her fifties who had terminal ovarian cancer. She knew she was "nearing her celestial discharge" from the hospital, as she candidly stated. Kathy had reflected with me on her life over a period of several days. Most meaningful to her as she neared the end of her life were the rituals she had treasured "growing up Catholic." Although she described herself as a non-practicing Catholic, who in her adult life struggled with certain aspects of Catholicism, Kathy respectfully fingered a tiny statue of the Sacred Heart of Jesus whenever we shared time together.

Increasingly, our visits were filled with Kathy's hope and plans for the things she could control in her dying process.

Increasingly, our visits were filled with Kathy's hopes

and plans for the things she could control in her dying process. Kathy began to consider ending her chemotherapy treatment and allowing herself to die naturally. She was "okay" with dying in the hospital rather than at home and had approved a "do not resuscitate" (DNR) order that would prevent extraordinary medical measures to revive her should her heart stop beating. The more Kathy talked about her "dying wishes" the more peaceful she became. And then one day, Kathy discussed the details of how she wanted her hospital room to look in the days preceding her death. Together, we meticulously outlined everything from the music of Chopin playing in the background to the blank journal for people to write in when they visited. As we talked, I wondered aloud if there were any religious symbols or rituals she would like to incorporate into her plan. She hesitated for a moment and then intently said, "Yes, I would like to be anointed." I was not surprised. The sacrament of the sick is often requested by practicing and lapsed Catholics alike. It is a ritual of comfort for both patient and family, and I knew the hospital priest who could be summoned when Kathy was ready.

After explaining the simple steps involved in fulfilling her request, Kathy's response surprised me. She shook her head and emphatically stated, "I don't want a priest to do it. I want *you* to do it." A lengthy dialogue ensued with me over-explaining to Kathy that I was neither ordained nor sanctioned in any way by the church to anoint her. She refused to accept my explanatory logic. Once again, Kathy insisted she was merely asking me, as her chaplain, to perform a ritual of anointing that could provide her peace and comfort.

In Kathy's case, I allowed my personal beliefs, biases, and fears to dictate my pastoral response to her. Although a part of me wanted to fulfill her request and provide Kathy with a meaningful ritual of anointing, I did not rest long enough in the space between stimulus and response. I told Kathy that because she was Catholic, only a priest could anoint her. She was visibly disappointed, declined the offer to have a priest anoint her, and became withdrawn after that conversation. What I realized later was the extent to which I had focused on the word *anoint;* how fearful I had been in my new role about making a wrong decision; and most importantly, that my CPE group and supervisor were readily available to discuss, process, and advise me on this type of dilemma; yet I had not reached out to them.

> *Kathy surprised me when she emphatically stated, "I don't want a priest to do it. I want YOU to do it."*

My next assigned shift started at 5:00 p.m. the following day. When I arrived at the hospital, I was briefed by the day on-call chaplain, and took the pager to start my fifteen-hour shift. Within ten minutes, the pager buzzed with the extension of the oncology unit. The nurse asked me to report to room 405 because a patient had just died. Stunned, I replied, "But that's Kathy's room." Her response was, "Yes. She just died." I could not believe Kathy was gone. Tears tumbled down my face onto my lap as I thought about Kathy, the hours we spent together planning for this, and my unwillingness to anoint her. It took several minutes to dry my tears, gather my thoughts, and breathe through my inability to forgive myself for not granting her final wish. "What was I afraid of?" I thought. "What did I do, or fail to do, for this precious woman?"

While I feel certain that Kathy has long ago forgiven me, I still believe that I deserted her when she really needed my pastoral presence. If the identical situation presented itself today, I would handle it differently. Years of experience have taught me about the permeability of some boundaries. Honoring Catholic tradition is not mutually exclusive to the sacramental nature of pastoral ministry. Sacraments are something Christians do, not just something that is done *to* them. These days, I define sacrament more broadly. I believe sacraments are those mystical, reflective moments that join people in a spirit of celebratory and transformational sharing.

Would I still inquire if the patient or family would prefer to have an ordained minister or priest perform the requested ritual? Absolutely, I would. Part of my role as chaplain is connecting the vulnerable with meaningful religious or spiritual resources. What I now understand more clearly is not to *exclude* myself as that resource, especially after the patient has *included* me. It was a valuable lesson learned at the expense of a patient's last wish.

Jewish Midrash, which is a collection of biblical commentaries and interpretations used to illustrate a moral principle, contrasts the words on a page with the white spaces surrounding them. The beauty of this concept is found in understanding how those who have lived and died speak to the present generation through the "silent white spaces between the words." Midrash invites the reader to listen for voices from the past to show the way to the future. It is a marvelous way of encouraging us to pay attention to the words on the paper while remaining open to all that the white space has to teach us. This lovely notion might be compared to living the *spirit of the law* versus the *letter of the law*, or could also serve as a reminder that life does not consist of rigid black and white boundaries, but is lived mostly in the grey areas. I think Midrash provides a deeper meaning by asking us to be mindful of and listen for the wisdom voices of our past experiences as well as those reflecting off the white

> *Jewish Midrash has a marvelous way of encouraging us to pay attention to the words on the paper while remaining open to all that the white space has to teach us.*

spaces around the text on every page of every good book. Maybe that is also what Viktor Frankl meant when he proffered his thoughts on the space between stimulus and response.

Being mindful of each situation as it unfolds, developing excellent assessment skills of patients' strengths and needs, recognizing any personal feelings that are being triggered, and remembering that our deepest desires as human beings are for connection, belonging, and relationship, serves me well as a chaplain. In every situation where boundaries exist, I privately and genuinely explore the question, "Whose needs are being met here?" Then I give myself the space to reflect, possibly consult a colleague, and consider both the safety of healthy boundaries and the boundlessness of compassion.

Mindfulness Prayer:

Boundless Love,

Come *walk with me* through the fertile fields of life; *and* come *sit awhile* with me *by the stream of* a thousand *difficult decisions.* Come *lift me* up *from* the anguish of *uncertainty* and *linger* with me *in the fragrant gardens* of justice; *and bask in* the sunlit terrain of *cultural sensitivity.* Come *hold my hand* and guide my feet toward the light of each new day; *and* then come *rest with me in the* spaciousness and *serenity of loving choices.* Come. *Open the windows of my heart.*

Amen.

Reflective Questions:

- Reread the entry poem to this chapter and consider what images or feelings about life that closed, locked, and open windows bring to mind.
- When, if ever, have you been confronted by your own lack of knowledge, or misinformation, about another culture? How did you handle the situation?
- How does your personal culture of values and beliefs inform the way in which you interact with those who differ? What are your steadfast boundaries? Which ones are more permeable?
- Can you think of an experience, perhaps like the one with Jeff, where you responded in a manner that may have seemed foreign to you, but you moved through it? How did it feel as you reflected on it afterward?
- What thoughts or feelings arose in you as you read about Kathy's request? How about my inability to fulfill, or the denial of, her final wish? How would you have handled Kathy's request?
- Although I mention that I am sure Kathy has long ago forgiven me, I do not say that I have forgiven myself. What is the significance of self-forgiveness in chaplaincy? In life?
- Consider a time when you crossed a boundary you knew you should not cross and the effect that decision had on you. What about a time when, after giving the stimulus more space and mindfulness, you moved forward with your response to cross or not to cross a boundary? What was the outcome?

Blessed are the mindful,

for they are keenly aware.

Chapter Seven

Be Collaborative

If you want to go quickly, go alone.
If you want to go far, go together.
-African proverb

Before you were born
did you deeply know....
Parents dedicated to kissing boo-boos to make them better
paced helplessly, prayed fervently,
unable to fix or provide what their tiny infant needed most?
Doctors and surgeons accustomed to healing
waited anxiously on indefinite hold for a phone call
releasing everyone from the bondage of delay?
Tiny humans wretched from the warmth of loving arms
connected to high-tech machines
keeping hearts pumping, blood flowing,
lungs expanding, contracting, meds dripping
like puzzles with missing pieces
desperately longing for the organ to make them whole again?
Before you were born did your sweet, selfless, spirit
collaborate with God?
Did you volunteer to become 'Jordan'
to save the tiny waiting ones with faulty parts?
And what of helpless bystander adults with hearts breaking
witnesses to your precious life cut short—
lived in four fleeting months?
Did you deeply know...
one day our distance from God
would grow shorter, closer, more meaningful?
Benefactors of your extraordinary collaboration
recipients of your boundless spirit—
all of us forever transformed by this experience of the heart!
Jordan, did you know?

No one can whistle a symphony.
It takes a whole orchestra to play it.
- H.E. Luccock

The concepts of heaven and hell have been preached about, debated, denied, upheld, taken for granted, and a source of concern for the dying since the dawn of Christianity. Some non-Christian religious traditions adhere to a belief in an afterlife and some do not. Some follow a theology of reincarnation, and some simply do not bother asking the question. As a chaplain who frequently ministers to people nearing the end of life, I have been privileged to bear witness to a broad spectrum of spiritual beliefs about heaven and hell.

One day, I came across a parable that resonated with me. According to this ancient teaching, a man was presented with an opportunity to glimpse both heaven and hell. He first stopped in hell, where the sight he witnessed was horrific. He saw row upon row of tables covered with every possible food delicacy. No spot on any table was empty. There was sumptuous food everywhere he looked; however, the people

> *As a chaplain, I have been privileged to bear witness to a broad spectrum of spiritual beliefs about heaven and hell.*

seated at the tables appeared withered, ravenous, and frail. They were moaning with hunger. Moving closer, the visitor observed that every person was holding eating utensils in both hands, but their arms were splinted so they could not bend their elbows to bring the delectable food to their mouths. The visitor cried at the dismal sight and tortuous sound of the pathetic people who had such succulent food nearby but could not taste or consume it.

Shortly after his glimpse of hell, the visitor arrived in heaven and was startled to see the identical setting he had witnessed in hell. Once again, there were rows of lengthy tables laden with delicious food. Conversely, in heaven the people around the tables were talking with one another and appeared satisfied from partaking of the abundant food. A closer look revealed that these people also had their arms splinted so they could not bend their elbows. Then he noticed a woman pick up her spoon, dig into the food in front of her, and stretch over the table to feed the person across from her. The recipient of her kindness then did likewise. The visitor stood in awe as he watched the collaborative efforts of each person feeding the other.

Reflecting further on this parable, what strikes me is the profound quality of its meaning. The single, but most significant, difference between heaven and hell is found in the participants' generous spirit of collaboration and cooperation. And every successful workplace environment understands the value of this parable's lesson.

Collaboration in a hospital environment involves a variety of disciplines. It also takes many twists and turns depending on each patient's current situation. Just five months into my career as a staff chaplain, I was privileged to participate in three of the most collaborative and poignant days of my life. All of the people involved owe their efforts and memories to a four-month-old infant named Jordan and his remarkable family: Tracey, Russell, and Mariah. With their permission, I share this story.

I was the chaplain assigned to the adult oncology, infant/toddler, school-age children, and pediatric intensive care (PICU) units. Valentine's Day was just around the corner. Children in the pediatric unit of the hospital were busy making valentines for loved ones. The day had been fairly quiet until one of the nurses in the PICU paged me. When I responded to the page, she asked me to come quickly, since an infant was being air-lifted to the hospital and was due to arrive momentarily.

Shortly after I got there, four-month-old Jordan arrived by helicopter and was rushed to the PICU. Nearly a dozen medical technicians were efficiently transferring his lifeless-looking body from the air flight apparatus to the monitors, tubes, and crib where he would spend the next three days. Because he could not breathe on his own, Jordan was connected to a ventilator. His mother, Tracey, waited anxiously for staff to complete the transfer so she could be closer to her tiny son. When I approached and introduced myself, Tracey collapsed into my arms sobbing from a deep inconsolable place within her. It was as if her heart was being crushed by dread. No words were exchanged and time seemed to stand still. I remember feeling as though someone else had swooped in to enfold us both. We just clung to one another as Tracey's grief poured out of her in an endless stream of tears.

> *When I introduced myself, Tracey collapsed into my arms sobbing from a deep inconsolable place within her.*

Finally, a PICU nurse gently tapped me on the shoulder and pointed to Jordan's room where monitors were softly beeping, and tiny Jordan lay connected to life-sustaining machines and medications. Tracey walked over and stood next to her son, gazing with disbelief. When she looked up and caught my eye, she pleaded, "Please tell me he's going to be alright." I knew I could not make that promise, but I did say, "That is certainly my prayer for Jordan and for you."

While waiting for Jordan's father, Russell, and his sister, Mariah, to make the three-hour drive from their home to the hospital, Tracey shared the story of her young family. Jordan was considered their "miracle baby" because he had been conceived a short while after Tracey's painful back surgery. Mariah was seven years old and thrilled to have a baby brother "to cuddle and fuss over." Tracey and Russell were so overjoyed with their recent arrival that they rarely left Jordan with baby-sitters. Then again, their jobs had recently changed, necessitating a modification to that protective environment.

Everything on this day was different. Jordan was staying with his grandparents. After his grandfather gently rocked Jordan to sleep, Jordan's grandmother did what many in the past have done when there was no crib available. She stacked pillows around the perimeter of an adult bed to ensure Jordan would not fall off and placed her sleeping grandson in the center. Tragically, on this day, another new thing occurred. Jordan rolled over for the first time; however, he did not roll off the bed. Instead, Jordan rolled from his back into a pillow. When his grandmother went to check on him, he was not breathing. Emergency medical services (EMS) was called immediately. They quickly arrived on the scene and managed to mechanically resuscitate Jordan, but no one knew exactly how long Jordan's young brain had been without oxygen. After an hour helicopter ride, he was lying in a PICU crib at our hospital and on life support. Preliminary test results indicated there was little chance for survival. Jordan's brain had been without oxygen too long.

The atmosphere in the PICU was incredibly sad. With

the arrival of Russell and Mariah, dialogue between medical staff and the family intensified as details were exchanged. A confused Mariah seemed lost among the questions, responses, tears, and technicians. When I noticed her clinging to Tracey's leg, I bent down to ask if she would like to stay in the room or come with me to make some valentines. Her face lit up like a summer sunrise. With a nod from her mother, Mariah grabbed my outstretched hand and skipped down the hall. When I pointed to the large silver button on the wall inside the PICU, she proudly pushed it granting us access to leave the intensive care unit.

Preliminary test results indicated there was little chance for survival. Jordan's brain had been without oxygen too long.

Soon we were standing outside the child life specialist's office. After a brief introduction and minimal details about how Mariah came to be at the hospital, Anna cheerfully handed Mariah several sheets of red construction paper, washable markers, and safety scissors. Before leaving Anna's office, I whispered that we might need her expertise with Mariah if Jordan did not survive. She nodded and handed me an emergency contact number.

Mariah and I located a quiet room where she could create valentines and safely ask her own questions about Jordan. She was age-appropriately inquisitive, only asking once what was wrong with her baby brother. Since Mariah's parents had not indicated what details to share with her, I kept my response honest but ambiguous. As Mariah colored, I informed her that Jordan was "very, very sick." I told her the doctors and nurses were doing everything they could to help him. It seemed that was all she needed. Immediately, Mariah wanted to make her first valentine for her baby brother. However, before completing her gift for Jordan, Mariah suddenly stopped, put down the scissors, and announced, "I want to go back and be with my brother." Her sudden shift surprised me, as she left her unfinished art work behind and began running down the hall. Moving swiftly after her, I wondered if Mariah felt a spiritual tug or sensed a silent call from Jordan. Arriving at the PICU doors a few steps before me, Mariah was anxiously slapping her hands against the closed doors. With tears in her eyes, she turned back and waved to me with a hurry-up motion. After swiping my badge to gain access to the PICU, the doors opened and Mariah rushed through. When I caught up with her, Mariah was standing next to Jordan's crib singing "Jesus Loves Me," replacing the word *me* with *you.* It was a tender, unforgettable moment.

When I caught up with her, Mariah was standing next to Jordan's crib singing "Jesus Loves Me."

Sadly, a few minutes later, I learned that test results revealed Jordan had no sign of brain activity. Everyone, including staff, was visibly distraught. The intensive care physician requested my presence as he explained the ominous news to Tracey and Russell. I quickly telephoned Anna, the child life specialist, asking her to come to the PICU. She seemed to arrive even before I could hang up the phone. Anna had a few toys in hand that caught Mariah's attention. The two of them moved to an empty room in the PICU, leaving Tracey and Russell alone with their son.

Gathering our emotional strength, Dr. Williams, Nurse Sonia, and I walked into Jordan's room. Tracey looked up and said, "It's bad, isn't it?" Dr. Williams nodded softly and pulled up a chair facing Jordan's parents. With a gentle voice and the kindest possible words, he began the difficult task of explaining the unbearable. Jordan's brain showed no signs of activity. All that was keeping the heart beating and oxygen moving through Jordan's tiny body were medications and machines. Grief-stricken, Tracey and Russell collapsed into each other's arms. Tears streamed down the distressed faces of everyone in the room. Asking if the parents would like some private time and receiving nods of assent, Dr. Williams, Nurse Sonia, and I stood up to leave. Tracey grabbed my arm and said, "Please stay with us."

Over the years, if chaplaincy has taught me anything, it is the myriad and individual ways grief manifests itself. Chaplaincy has also taught me how to listen and sit with grief, rather than attempt to fix it. Due to inexperience, I was strongly tempted to speak words of comfort, but I instinctively knew that comfort was an impossible goal, and I bravely kept silent. Tracey and Russell were grieving, and they needed someone to honor their grief with quiet compassion. At some point, Russell looked at Tracey, then at me and tearfully inquired, "What do we do now?" Chaplains know there are questions that seek answers and there are questions that require further exploration. Russell's question seemed like the latter, so I responded, "What would *you* like to do now?" After a long pause and reflective looks at each other, Russell asked if they must make a decision about removing Jordan from life-support. I felt these parents needed more time before such a seemingly impossible decision could be made. I assured Russell and Tracey that while no amount of time would be enough, they would not be rushed by any of us. This reassurance seemed to give them some immediate relief.

> *Chaplains know there are questions that seek answers and some that require further exploration.*

I was aware that in situations like Jordan's, the organ donor team would be called in to speak with the family about options. I also knew they preferred to address this sensitive topic with families rather than have the chaplain bring it up; therefore, I had not mentioned organ donation to Jordan's parents. Later that afternoon, when the organ donor team arrived to have this conversation with Tracey and Russell, I was invited to be there as a supportive presence. The two members of the team were remarkably compassionate. They began with heart-felt expressions of empathy for the parents and regret for the dreadful tragedy the family was facing. After discussing the organ donor program and process, they gave Tracey and Russell some private time to decide whether they wanted to share their son's organs with others in need. Learning that Jordan might possibly save the life of one or more infants through the tragedy of his own death seemed to bring a small amount of comfort to Tracey and Russell. After further contemplation, they agreed to allow the donor team to proceed.

Learning that Jordan might possibly save the life of one or more infants through the tragedy of his own death seem to bring a small amount of comfort to his parents.

Once Russell and Tracey made their decision, the organ donation team began the pain-staking and collaborative process of locating matches for Jordan's organs. Organ donation regulations can vary from state to state. Generally, detailed information about the donor and recipients is kept confidential. However in this case, the prospective recipient of Jordan's heart was a high-profile child on the opposite side of the country; therefore, the team decided Jordan's parents needed to be informed. No names, cities, or hospitals were provided—just that it was a high-profile case. Jordan's liver, kidneys, other organs, and tissue would help save a total of seven local children, but his heart would be flown across the country.

On the evening of the third day, we were told the transport team was due to arrive around 11:00 p.m. Jordan would be taken to surgery when the cross-country team entered the hospital. Everything depended upon precise timing. The heart could be sustained outside of Jordan's body for a maximum of five hours. It would take the transport team just under that amount of time to make the flight to the waiting infant. Meanwhile, I began preparing the family for their final night with Jordan. Aunts, uncles, grandparents, sister, and parents were all gathered in Jordan's room.

Over the course of several hours, Tracey, Russell, and I discussed how they wished to say good-bye to Jordan. Ultimately, they chose to have a "blessing and sending forth" ceremony in Jordan's room just before he went to surgery. PICU nurses who were deeply touched by this remarkable family asked if they could attend. Graciously, Jordan's parents agreed, and at 10:45 p.m. we began our intimate service with a life-supported Jordan being placed in his mother's arms. Mariah held a small sea-shell containing anointing oil. Everyone in the room participated. Each

> *As she anointed Jordan with oil, she whispered, "Some people take a lifetime to fulfill their purpose. Some only take four months."*

person, beginning with Tracey, touched the oil, blessed Jordan, and offered a personal prayer. Some mentioned ways this precious infant had touched their life. Others expressed their love and grief. One person made a statement I will always remember. While anointing Jordan with oil, she whispered, "Some people take a lifetime to fulfill their purpose. Some only take four months." Drawing the ceremony to a close with a chorus of "Somewhere Over the Rainbow," a staff member opened the door to let us know that the transport team had arrived. We walked in procession, ushering Jordan's crib down the hallway toward the surgical area. The moments before Jordan disappeared through the surgery room doors were heartrending when Tracey, Russell, and Mariah said good-bye to their "miracle baby" one last time. Walking them to their car later, I thought, "These are the bravest people I have ever known."

Jordan's story of collaboration did not end with the surgery. In the weeks following his funeral, new events began unfolding. When Jordan's maternal aunt learned about the donation of his heart to a "high-profile case," she began searching the Internet and discovered infant twins who were awaiting heart transplants. The same day Jordan's heart was flown across the country, newspapers reported that a heart match had been found for one of the twins. Enough details about time and transportation concerns were published to make a logical connection. News media were closely following the twins' story and reported on the power of organ donation to save lives. In her anguish, Tracey's sister was further grieved that no mention was made of her family's generosity in donating the life-saving heart to one of the twins. She contacted the media voicing her disappointment and despair.

Before long, news media were contacting Jordan's family. Approval was sought and given for both donor and recipient families to meet. Tracey, Russell, and Mariah were flown across the country to meet the family whose infant had been saved by Jordan's heart donation. According to Tracey's later account, the meeting between families was emotionally-charged. Tears of gratitude mixed with tears of joy and sadness flowed like a never-ending river. Each family brought small but meaningful gifts to exchange, one of which was a tiny, heart-shaped silver box. A pivotal and poignant moment occurred when Tracey was offered a stethoscope so she could listen to her son's heart beating in the recipient infant's chest. Through a flood of tears, Tracey listened, feeling both intense sorrow and incredible joy. On the flight home, she and Russell shared how they were comforted in knowing that Jordan lives on in such a very special way.

> *A pivotal and poignant moment occurred when Tracey was offered a stethoscope so she could listen to her son's heart beating in another infant's chest.*

Listening by phone to Tracey's re-telling of the encounter, I was profoundly moved by these families' shared experiences. Later, both families also appeared on *Good Morning America* and in a *People* magazine article. Although neither Tracey nor Russell sought or expected notoriety from Jordan's tragic death, they became thankful for the opportunity to educate others on the impact and importance of organ donation. The recipient family was elated their baby would survive through the gracious gift of donation. Nevertheless, Jordan's family, despite the peace-filled feeling donating his organs brought them, were still desperately grieving the loss of their infant son. Russell, Tracey, and Mariah wanted everyone to understand the emotional elements involved. All these years later, they continue to be strong, faith-filled advocates for organ donation and are extremely grateful for the chance to have shared both sides of the organ donation story.

A few years later, Tracey, Russell, and Mariah's family grew by one as they welcomed baby Jazmyne into the world. We periodically check-in via phone calls and social media. On every occasion of reconnection, my heart seems to skip a beat as I think of Jordan and hear his family's ongoing story of remembrance and recovery.

Jordan's story resonates with me as a lesson in collaboration. Everyone doing what they were trained for contributed to the transformative power of this tragedy. The

EMS team, PICU staff, child life specialist, chaplain, organ donor team, all behind-the-scenes organ technicians searching files for matches, surgical teams at both donor and recipient sites, transport crew, and most especially, Jordan's family, transformed a tragedy into a life-giving experience. That I was able to witness and take an active role in the process left me deeply humbled. A tiny red heart on the front of my driver's license indicates that I am an organ donor. That little mark on my license is a constant reminder of Jordan and his gift of life.

Jordan was my introduction to the intense ministry of pediatric chaplaincy. I recall feeling inadequate and unequipped for the vital work I was thrown into the day Jordan and his family came into my life. And yet, every hour of the three days I spent with this family provided endless opportunities for learning and growth. I also trusted the skills I had acquired from my year-long CPE residency and did not shy away from the family's or the staff's needs for and appreciation of my non-anxious presence in their midst.

In retrospect, there are a few things I would do differently. While my immediate ministry to the family was appropriate and helpful, I would have worked more closely with the social worker to provide Tracey, Russell, Mariah, and other members of the family with grief counseling resources. Thankfully, they did seek such help on their own. These days, through another collaborative effort, bereavement packets have been tastefully designed and constructed for families when they leave the hospital after a death. The packets contain vital information loved ones may need for funeral planning, lists of local funeral homes, signs and symptoms of grief, grief counseling, support group lists, and contact information for all staff members who were with them during their time at the hospital. Families often comment on the insight these bereavement packets provided for them.

> *The interdisciplinary work of patient care calls each member of the team to bring individual skills and information to the table in a spirit of cooperation, collaboration, and collegiality.*

Someone once said, "It's heaven all the way to heaven and it's hell all the way to hell." Similar to the parable of heaven and hell shared at the beginning of this story, kindness expressed through collaboration transforms the environment. Because personal needs or ego can interfere with any transformational process, asking the soul-searching question, "What motivates me in this circumstance?" can be personally revealing and therefore transformative. The interdisciplinary work of patient care implores each member of the team to bring individual skills and information to the table in a spirit of cooperation, collaboration, and collegiality. When this happens, even in the most challenging situations, outcomes are improved for everyone involved.

Collaboration Prayer:

Spirit of Oneness,

May all creation *sing* unending rhythms of harmony *into my heart* when I feel connected and especially when I feel disconnected. May *songs of cooperation* stimulate my personal and professional goals. May *melodies of collaboration* rejuvenate my weary spirit. May *themes of interdependence* stir my imagination toward peaceful solutions.

And as I celebrate my own unique contributions, may *the music of unity* remind me of the healing quality of working alongside kindred spirits as co-laborers in the shared ministry of love, *always for the greater good of the world.* Amen.

Reflective Questions:

- In the parable of heaven and hell, what do you think motivates the people in heaven to help each other? What prevents those in hell from doing the same?
- What feelings about organ donation surfaced as you read Jordan's story?
- What is our role as chaplains with family members when they are faced with the difficult decision of organ donation? What about the chaplains' role with the organ donor team?
- How would you respond if a family member asked for your input on the decision to donate a loved one's organs?
- Do you think the decision to visit the child and family that received the donor heart was healing for the parents? If so, how would you prepare or counsel a family who was about to make such a journey?
- How would you explain Mariah's sudden desire to go see her brother? Reflect on your personal comfort level with the grief of young siblings and ways to support them. Consider reading books on this topic such as Pastoral Care with Children in Crisis by Andrew D. Lester and The Secret Spiritual World of Children by Tobin Hart and Joseph Chilton Pearce.
- How do you collaborate with co-workers in your current career? Has there ever been a time when you were tempted to *not* collaborate with co-workers? What was the result?

- If you could change one thing about the way collaboration works or does not work in your place of employment, what would it be? Why would you change it? How would you go about facilitating change?

Blessed are the collaborative,

for they are co-laborers in healing.

Chapter Eight

Be Authentic

We begin to find and become ourselves
when we notice how we are already found,
already truly, entirely, wildly, messily,
marvelously who we were born to be.
- Anne Lamott

Your life is a book with far too few chapters;
remember that meaning is found in the pictures and words of every page.

Living is like reading a book;
never turn to the next page until you are very sure you have taken in everything
where you are right now.

Give all you have to playing the game or toy you hold;
push every button, wait for the music, and then let the rhythm move through you.

Food is more than mere bodily nourishment;
each morsel can be an exploration of variety,
texture, taste, and satisfaction.
So, eat what you enjoy, enjoy what you eat, and in no particular order—broccoli is as good for breakfast
as strawberries are for dessert.

Call it what it is;
if someone tries to pull the wool over your eyes,
humor them at first,
but ultimately stand your ground—
a duck is a duck, not a dinosaur.

Employ humor when entertaining visitors;
allow others to act silly as a way of inviting them into your space to enjoy a good laugh—
it brings out the best in both of you.

Trust deeply in the love of others;
they will permit you to do for yourself what you can and be close enough to support and sustain you when you simply cannot.

And every so often let people do something for you that you know you can do for yourself—
because they need to.

Give voice to your needs;
no visitor, parent, family member, caregiver, or well-intentioned person can read your mind—
no matter how much they love you and you love them.

Forgive everyone—everyday;
start each morning with a clean slate, forgiving all the things done to you the previous day—
forgiveness is the balm of healing.

Always remember the scars you carry have healing potential.

Rest when the events of the day
take a toll on your body, mind, and spirit.
Sleep is a natural healer. Your words of wisdom on this subject still resonate:
"I love a good nap!!"

Today you are you! That is truer than true!
There is no one alive who is you-er than you!
- Dr. Seuss

Maybe you have seen it too. There is a program on public television called *Antiques Roadshow* that I find positively mesmerizing. In the show, appraisal experts travel to major cities around the country, where citizens bring in treasured or merely sentimental objects to determine their financial worth. I have often been surprised by the high appraisal value assigned to many of the items people find in their attics, cellars, homes, and storage units. Watching from the comfort of my home, I am sometimes fooled by the appearance of an object that I am sure could not be valuable, only to find out from the experts that a metal penny bank is priceless. Something as simple as a toy train locomotive or as delicate as an intricately painted vase can be valued at thousands of dollars, depending on such things as the condition, artist, number created, and age. Yet, regardless of whether the article is a painting, a wood carving, an old book, or something I might not even recognize, its assessed value depends heavily on its undisputed authenticity. Owners are told on the spot if their object is a reproduction. To put it simply, no copy has the same value as its original.

The first time I watched *Antiques Roadshow*, I thought about how people also need to be authentic and how beautifully children demonstrate this quality. One of the joys I experience working with young children is witnessing their uninhibited approach to living. Quite frequently, I have been privileged to engage children in conversations about their opinions on life. More often, the children captivate me with their candid, unsolicited comments. I am always pleasantly surprised by their complete absence of pretense. If being authentic means being genuine and real, then young children are living examples of authenticity. They regularly speak the truth as they understand it and often display a willingness to disclose their most unabridged perceptions of life. There is no doubt children have blessed me with moments of illuminating insight and irrepressible laughter. Eli was one of those children.

Eli was born with numerous medical anomalies, one of which required open heart surgery shortly after his birth. The list of medical abnormalities was long and significant. But, what was wrong with Eli did not define him as much as what was magnificently right with him. Having spent the majority of his first months of life in the hospital, Eli's personality developed before the eyes of his clinical team. Because he moved from unit to unit based on what had recently been done to and for him, this included most of the hospital staff. Immediately following his birth, Eli was in the neonatal intensive care unit (NICU). When he had undergone additional surgery, he was in the pediatric intensive care unit. Once stabilized and on the healing path after surgery, Eli might be found in the intermediate care unit (IMC) or the medical/surgical unit (Med/Surg). By the time he was two, nearly everyone at the hospital knew and loved Eli.

Those of us who knew Eli well, often described him as an "old soul," which was a title bestowed by the staff on those rare children who seemed wise beyond their years. Practically from the time he was born, we noticed and commented on Eli's enigmatic smile. When Eli looked into my eyes, I had the unexplainable feeling he could see into my soul. I was not alone in that line of thinking. Other staff members reported feeling the same way. I also sensed a deep knowingness in Eli. One day, when Eli's mother, Abigail, and I were talking, I mentioned this to her. We pondered the notion that the spirit of Eli had long ago *volunteered* to be born in this less-than-perfect body in order to bring the rest of us closer to God. The concept appeared to give Abigail both a sense of wonder and a feeling of peace. Whenever I think of Eli, the smile that ripples across

It seemed Eli had received an abundance of brain cells to make up for all the glitches that ravaged his body.

my face assures me this idea must be true.

Many characteristics about Eli made him unique. Red hair, distinctive by its vibrant color and straight-as-an-arrow, wild appearance, was just one of his trademarks. If I was down thc hall and out of sight from Eli's room, I could often hear his youthful belly laugh as he entertained visitors who mistakenly thought *they* were amusing him. Eli's mental capabilities were so acute that it seemed he had received an abundance of brain cells to make up for all the glitches that ravaged his body.

Books were special treasures to Eli. Whether reading a Dr. Seuss book quietly by himself or being read to by someone else, Eli had a meditative approach to books. Neither he nor the person reading to him was permitted to turn a page until Eli had taken in every detail. This process was remarkable to watch. If anyone turned a page before he was ready, Eli would reach over and flip the page back as if to say, "Hey, are you sure we're done with that part of the story?" He was not even two years old and yet Eli studied every page of every book as if it were a guide for living life to the fullest. Whenever I read a book to Eli, I had the distinct feeling there was something on each page he wanted *me* to notice. Right there on the pages of *Green Eggs and Ham* or in a wordless book of pictures, *I* was supposed to learn something about life. Eli taught me to pause and notice the words, the illustrations, and maybe more importantly, the space around them.

Watching Eli play was a treat to behold. Most youngsters seem to love toys for the magical entertainment quality they possess. But Eli had a penchant for simple toys, especially musical ones, and their ability to imitate life. The way in which he inspected a plaything—new or old—was mystical. Eli would sit for hours scrutinizing a single object as if inviting it into relationship with him, or vice versa. Before long, Eli would begin pushing any obvious buttons. When his favorite *Talking Elmo* toy responded with words, Eli smiled like he and the Muppet were in deep conversation with one another. If pressing a button resulted in music, Eli listened intently at first and then methodically and repeatedly pressed the button until he absorbed the message of the music. Ultimately, while everyone around him listened to a childhood tune, Eli moved his body gently in rhythm as if hearing a classical Mozart concert. Eli intrigued me with his uncanny ability to authentically enjoy every moment, without regard for who might be watching him and what they might be thinking. He was just being Eli.

> *Eli would sit for hours scrutinizing a single toy as if inviting it into relationship with him.*

On the other hand, not every day of Eli's life was spent in the hospital. From time to time, he would be well enough to go home for a few days or weeks. This was cause for great celebration by his older brother, parents, and grandparents. We all rejoiced with his family on the occasions of Eli's discharge. And even though he seemed to thrive in the hospital, according to his mother, Eli was decidedly more jubilant on the rides home. Abigail often shared how much Eli enjoyed life, whether he was riding through the hospital in a wagon, sitting in his car seat on the way home, or hanging out with family. Eli seemed to have been born with a knack for focusing on the wonder of life rather than on the challenges life presented.

Then one early spring day, just before his third birthday, Eli was once again admitted to the hospital. This time, his symptoms were notably different. Sadly, tests revealed tumors in several locations of Eli's body, including his head. Eli was diagnosed with lymphoma. Because radiation to the brain is never a good option for children under three years of age, brain surgery was scheduled and performed. Eli's ability to tolerate the countless assaults on his little body amazed even the most stoic staff. One surgeon commented that while Eli's body was struggling to heal after a surgery, his soulful eyes seemed to indicate that he understood and forgave everyone on the team for any pain inflicted on him. I remember being present one morning as he was being bathed and dressed for the

> *"God," I prayed, "how much more does this child have to endure? Please help him."*

day. Eli's little body was riddled with scars from open heart surgery, gastric surgery, and chest tubes. Now he had another scar on his head. "God," I prayed, "how much more does this child have to endure? Please help him." Later when I stopped by the hospital chapel to pray for Eli, it was like God whispered, "I *am* helping Eli. Look around and notice all the people I've sent to help. Eli sure has noticed everyone—including you!"

Once again, Eli bounced back from surgery only to face the next assault on his body. This time, it was in the form of chemotherapy, which of course, he tolerated better than most. Eli also had a new mark of distinction. Brain surgery left a significant scar behind his ear and also caused slight nerve damage to the side of his face. When Eli smiled, or more likely broke into a belly laugh, the right side of his mouth did not curve up to match the left side. Almost as though he knew his crooked smile was a new characteristic to show off, Eli inconceivably seemed to smile more after his surgery than he had before.

One of my trademarks as a pediatric chaplain was a small plastic yellow duck attached to my identification badge. When I pushed the button on the top of its head, a light shot out from its beak and the duck made a peculiar quacking sound. Most children under five years of age knew me by my duck rather than by my title. I found this a fun way to be identified, gain permission from children to enter their rooms, build trust, and employ humor. However, with Eli, this duck became a game we played together. I would ask him what animal it was, and as if I were the student and he the teacher, Eli would gently remind me it was a duck. Once, and only once, when I asked Eli what the duck was, he outrageously replied, “A dinosaur!” With his red hair waving wildly, he broke into the loudest, longest-lasting, most intense belly laugh I had ever heard. His laugh was so spontaneous and contagious that within a few seconds I was laughing hysterically right along with him. Others outside his room came in to see what was so funny, and without explanation, they too became caught up in the laughter. Minutes later, everyone in the room felt the euphoria brought on by laughter that Eli had jump-started. To this day, I believe Eli knew exactly what he was doing when he called my duck a dinosaur. From that day forward, when I asked Eli if my duck was a dinosaur, he would politely correct me by stating, “It’s not a dinosaur. It’s a duck!” Eli knew the spontaneous moment with the duck had passed and it was time to get back to reality. Yet, he still looked at me with those soulful eyes and offered a crooked little smile in acknowledgement of my attempt to humor him. Eli exuded hospitality.

During one of his stays in the pediatric intensive care unit, Eli began showing signs of battle fatigue. When he was strong enough, he would sit in his crib surrounded by a variety of foods he loved. Sometimes he would take a bite of strawberry ice cream and then move to a piece of broccoli or macaroni and cheese. True to his nature, Eli examined each morsel inviting his body to reveal what it needed in the moment. In the midst of his persistent independence, Eli also began to trust others to help him. Even when he could do something for himself, Eli demonstrated an unconditional love for those who had cared for him by permitting *us* to do small things for *him*. Once again, this young but very wise child gave to others what he perceived we needed.

For several months, the oncology team desperately attempted to eradicate lymphoma from Eli's body. Try as he did to continue his ordained role as poster child for hospitality, Eli slowly grew sicker and less physically able to enjoy life. Even in his final hours, a mostly unresponsive Eli hung on, making certain that each family member, nurse, physician, child life specialist, surgeon, and chaplain who had loved and been loved by him were afforded an opportunity to say good-bye. Finally, with his mother lying next to him in bed, and without opening his eyes, Eli turned to kiss her on the cheek. His last words were, "It's okay, mom."

In the days following Eli's death, I spent hours at the computer struggling to find words to describe the impact of his three brief years of life. Suddenly, late one evening, I felt Eli's presence with me. He was smiling his crooked little smile and almost seemed to be laughing at me for making his eulogy so difficult. I closed my eyes, sat very still with the sweetest image of Eli in my mind, and realized that Eli was encouraging me to tell those attending his memorial service what I had learned from him. When I opened my eyes and began typing, the words came easily and swiftly. I could almost hear Eli's belly laugh as we revisited a few of the humorous moments in his short life. Without much effort, words flew onto the page. Soon I noticed it was my own laughter I was hearing. But I knew Eli was there in spirit. His presence was palpable. Some of what I wrote and delivered at his service became a poem I titled "Lessons from Eli" and appears at the beginning of this chapter. Whenever I read the poem, I feel the presence of a wise, red-headed toddler who is most assuredly at peace and creating joy with his authentic personality and genuine belly laugh.

I could almost hear Eli's belly laugh as we revisited a few of the humorous moments in his short life.

What are the lessons for chaplains in Eli's journey? Scarred from surgeries too numerous to count, Eli was nevertheless comfortable in his own skin. He seemed to know his scars were part of who he was, and yet through these very scars his personality came to life. For chaplains, there is simply no better tool available than knowing who we are as persons before we come to chaplaincy. Awareness of our strengths and weaknesses offers a pathway to growth opportunities. Looking honestly into our personal wounds and scars creates a fountain of compassion from which we serve others.

Most importantly, authentic use of self generates a space for relationship to grow by establishing the conditions for honest communication at a profound level—physically, emotionally, and spiritually. Sometimes in my early days of training, I shadowed other chaplains by observing their pastoral skills in patients' rooms. I recall thinking that I might need to mimic the techniques I witnessed. Then one day, it struck me that what I was noticing was the chaplain's personality shining through her skills. At that moment, I decided to allow my personality to be the sharpest tool on my chaplain tool belt. Weeks later, while browsing through a bookstore I found and purchased a paperweight that sits on my desk to remind me of this discovery. Every morning I read and smile at Oscar Wilde's quotation of sound advice: "Be yourself. Everyone else is taken."

The lessons from Eli's short life are plentiful and powerful. Eli taught me the priceless lesson of living in the moment by staying on a single page of life, taking in all it has to offer before moving on to the next. By watching Eli, I learned there will always be countless distractions seeking attention, but nothing is as important as being attentive to the here and now. Then, despite what life tosses our way, we must not take ourselves too seriously. Eli would want each of us to remember that laughter lightens the heaviest of burdens and appropriate use of humor does a body good.

Authenticity Prayer:

Mystical Reality,

The world is not an easy place to walk as my true self. *Distractions* of false gods *tempt me to* put on masks that *hide who I really am*. Remind me daily that you *love me* as I am. You do not ask me to be an improved version of someone else. You *call me to the table of authenticity,* to be the person you created me to be. *Breathe in me* breath of God. *That I may live* and breathe and have my being in you, please live and breathe and have your being in me. *Shine your light of genuine love* on me so *that I may,* in turn, *radiate* your goodness, the Divine DNA of *authenticity*, toward everyone I meet, and especially toward myself. Amen.

Reflective Questions:

- What feelings and images come to mind when you reflect on being authentic? What about a time when you may have been insincere?
- How difficult or simple is it for you to be genuine in thought, word, and deed? When is it difficult? When is it simple? Why?
- What made Eli different from other children his age? Have you known a child similar to Eli? What have you learned from that child?
- What thoughts did you have about the concept of Eli's spirit offering to come into the world in a less-than-perfect body to bring others closer to God?
- What "Lessons from Eli" can you derive from the message of the opening poem? If you were to write your own "Lessons from ______," what would the message be?
- How does Eli's approach to reading books inspire you to savor the preciousness of each moment?
- What makes you the person you are? What are your characteristics of authenticity?
- What does *authentic use of self* mean to you?

Blessed are the authentic,

for they are genuinely relational.

Chapter Nine

Be Wise

We delight in the beauty of the butterfly, but rarely admit the changes it has gone through to achieve that beauty.
- Maya Angelou

Native Americans call the rain *female* when
air is motionless and gentle beads of water
fall steadily from peaceful clouds
soaked up instantly by the awaiting thirsty ground.
Sometimes when I pay close attention
Sophia [Wisdom] pours over me
like a female rain gently bathing the desert
and I, too, soak her up.
Occasionally she arrives without warning
like a ray of winter sunshine breaking through
an otherwise dreary day of burdensome snowfall.
Once in a while she brushes past me
with the excitement of a newly hatched butterfly
revealing her knowledge in explosive color.
Often she sits quietly in moonlit shadows
as we search for meaning
in the unspeakable darkness of life.
But then, unexpectedly, she joins me
in uncontrollable giggles
as if we had just eaten an entire meal
of baby belly-laughs.
Ah! sweet *Sophia!*

Ah! sweet ***Wisdom!***

You yourself, as much as anybody in the entire universe deserve your love and affection.
- Buddha

My heart feels heavy. I grieve, along with the rest of the country, and perhaps the entire world, the lives of twenty first-graders and six adults massacred in the morning hours of their day at Sandy Hook Elementary School in Connecticut. I watched in disbelief as details of the unspeakable carnage unfolded. My eyes were glued to the television for two days, waiting expectantly for some rational explanation to make sense of this most heinous act of violence. None will be forthcoming. At least no explanation will be offered sufficient to assuage the inconsolable suffering of families and neighbors whose loved ones were killed, or those of us who grieve from a distance.

The evening after the slaughter of innocent lives, I watched a few community spokespersons respond to media interviews. One of the people who caught my attention was Fr. Robert Weiss, the priest from St. Rose of Lima Roman Catholic Church. Fr. Weiss accompanied police as parents were notified of their children's deaths in the school shootings. He spoke of the tragedy: how the community was coming together in supportive prayer vigils and of the eight funerals to be held in his church alone. Breaking down with emotion, Fr. Weiss turned from the camera to someone standing behind him, but the microphone caught his barely audible words: "I'm so tired."

Instantly, I knew Fr. Weiss was not complaining. Instead, he was attempting to offer a reason for his on-camera emotional breakdown. Being one of the spiritual leaders of the community, Fr. Weiss may have had expectations that somehow in the process of being supportive he also needed to hold everything together. While it would be presumptuous of me to say I understand how he was feeling, I do presume to know that in the midst of this dreadful crisis, there will be little, if any, time for Fr. Weiss to care for himself. The prayer list I created for families of the deceased immediately grew longer. I added Fr. Weiss, and the lone funeral director, all the other unnamed spiritual leaders, first responders, and volunteer grief counselors in the tiny community of Sandy Hook. The ministry of caregiving can take a physical, emotional, and spiritual toll on a person.

Women and men who feel called to chaplaincy often express their calling in terms of helping others find meaning in the midst of life's most challenging events. This concept also appears to be true in many healthcare professions such as nursing, social work, and counseling. Whenever I have asked my peers how they came to choose chaplaincy as a profession, I learned that one or more significant life events triggered the interest and ultimately, the sense of calling. In my case, the situation was no different. The death of my dear friend Judy became the catalyst for a career in chaplaincy. Judy's simple request that I do something for hospice turned into her perpetual gift. Rarely does a day pass without a reflective thought on the transformational quality hidden within my friendship and spiritual journey with Judy. Instead of being a final journey, Judy lives on daily in the countless people I meet in my chaplain ministry.

Judy's simple request that I do something for hospice turned into her perpetual gift.

Discovering the deeper reasons why people are drawn to careers in helping professions is beyond the scope of this book. Nonetheless, as with many aspects of life, I can presume that both nature and nurture play a role. We are born with certain inherited tendencies and personality characteristics. Our life experiences transform us. Like a chrysalis morphing into a butterfly, human challenges and choices, joys and sorrows, along with our responses, begin to shape and transform us into the person we become.

Once the call to chaplaincy and our response occurs, the next salient question is less about *why* than it is about *how*. How do we keep the wellspring of compassion from drying up while we devote our lives and extend our energy toward assisting others?

Wisdom in chaplaincy involves being a good steward of the unique gifts chaplains bring to the table of healthcare. Stewardship requires that we strike a healthy balance between being present to the needs of patients, families, and staff while still honoring our own physical, spiritual, and emotional needs. Simply stated, we cannot be a healthy presence and benefit to people in crisis if we do not renew, refill, and restore ourselves along the way. How can we possibly adequately assess and advocate for others if we are unable or unwilling to do so for ourselves?

Without question, a challenging part of being a chaplain revolves around knowing when to stay and when to leave a given situation. Several colleagues and I have termed this as the "know when to hold them, when to fold them, and when to walk away" syndrome. All pastoral visits, especially those involving crisis, require ongoing assessment skills to determine if the patient and family members are still in need of a pastoral presence. Would they be comfortable with another chaplain stepping in to finish? Are they capable of moving forward on their own? Furthermore, and most

> *Wisdom in chaplaincy involves being a good steward of the unique gifts chaplains bring to the table of healthcare.*

significantly, as chaplains we need to assess what may or may not be motivating us to stay or leave the current situation.

The CPE residency program taught me the importance of asking patients or family members if it is time for me to leave. At some point, when it appears the patient is calmer or more comfortable with the particular situation, I may ask, "Are you ready for some private time?" Some have replied, "Yes," while others have surprised me with a response of, "Please don't go yet." There have also been times in the evening when I needed to turn the situation over to the on-call chaplain because I was certain the need for pastoral care was going to extend far beyond the hours I was available.

For example, a few years ago on Thanksgiving Day, I had volunteered to be the sole chaplain on afternoon duty. The hospital had been especially quiet. I toured every unit in the building to check on other staff members working the holiday. It was nearing 3:00 p.m., so I headed to my office to tie up loose ends and complete any paperwork before heading home for a turkey dinner with waiting family and friends. The evening on-call chaplain was scheduled to be available at 4:30 p.m. Just as I began to unlock the office door, my pager went off. A trauma victim was on his way to the emergency room with injuries from a traffic accident. The estimated arrival time was ten minutes.

When I entered the ER, the helicopter was still en route. I noticed two people dressed in local college team colors walking toward me. The young woman was fingering rosary beads. They grabbed me and asked if their cousin had arrived yet. I told them he was on his way via helicopter and commented that they must live nearby to have arrived so quickly. The woman held up her rosary and said, "We live two decades away." I smiled, inwardly thinking that I had heard of distance being described in terms of miles or measure of time, but never by number of rosary decades. I gently ushered them to a family consultation room to await the arrival of their loved one. They shared the details of the accident as they understood them. Several out-of-town family members were on their way to attend a college football game when their sports utility vehicle (SUV) flipped over, throwing one of the passengers out. Apparently, everyone else in the car was safe. This couple had no idea how serious their cousin's injuries were. Anxiously, they asked me to pray the rosary with them.

I had never heard travel distance defined by number of decades of a rosary.

Shortly after we began praying the rosary, the air flight team arrived. Other family members also began pouring into the ER. Leaving the family for a brief time to seek information on the condition of the victim, I was told by the attending ER physician to "stay close because this does not look good." Within minutes the patient was stabilized and taken to surgery for repair of his substantial head injuries. Armed with the knowledge that the patient would be moved to the intensive care unit after surgery, I accompanied the numerous family members to the larger ICU waiting area. At about 7:00 p.m., with the family still waiting for the patient to return from surgery, I inquired if they were ready for some "alone time." Several family members looked at me and seemed to silently plead, "Don't leave us. We're scared." But the woman with the rosary jumped up, threw her arms around me, and said, "You've been an angel to us. Now that we're all together, I think we'll be okay." At their request, we gathered in a circle for prayer, after which I assured them of the on-call chaplain's availability. I also mentioned that I would be working the next day and would check on them first thing in the morning.

Questions that were asked and discussed among staff chaplains in the days following this trauma fell under the categories of self-care and patient care. Initially, the topic was self-care *versus* patient care, but one wise person in the group astutely observed that the two were not mutually exclusive and should be discussed in that light. Interestingly, we concluded that I did the best thing for the traumatized family by remaining available to the family as they awaited the results of surgery. Even though I took time to notify my own family that I would be delayed, they chose to hold dinner until I arrived and were hungry and tired by the time I got home. Most of the staff chaplains felt I *could* have (not necessarily *should* have) turned the trauma over to the on-call chaplain a little sooner—as a measure of self-care. Everyone agreed that chaplains make these decisions in the moment and must be trusted to do what seems best at the time—for the patient and their family as well as for themselves and their own family. Like many things in life, the wisdom of personal experience often comes through trial and error; however, seeking the counsel of skilled colleagues is invaluable in decision-making processes.

One wise person observed that self-care and patient care are not mutually exclusive terms.

The trauma patient survived surgery and spent several days in the ICU before being transported to a rehabilitation facility. Recovery was slow and arduous, but steady progress was made. Every year since the trauma, I receive a Thanksgiving Day card, note of thanks, or a family photo from the *Rosary Lady*, showing me how well her cousin is doing since the accident. I always share these gracious mementos with my family who waited without complaint for me to join them that Thanksgiving Day long ago.

In each of the previous chapters, I selected one story from my years as a chaplain to convey a component, or be-attitude of chaplaincy. Although some of the stories are particularly unique, they are only a sampling from thousands. I have never left work thinking that I experienced a boring or uneventful day. Instead, the days overflow with more needs than I am capable of tending to, and so necessitate making choices to help me maintain the balance of nurturing others and myself.

The story of Mr. Q in chapter two underscores how, despite my internal desire to run away, I was able to assess that leaving him to deal with his anxiety alone would have been both insensitive and unprofessional. Noticing my feelings of inadequacy and moving through them opened a space for both Mr. Q and me to learn valuable lessons. Stuart's story of self-forgiveness in chapter three is a story that also highlights what a difference it made for me, as the chaplain familiar with Stuart's history, to stay with him in spite of the clock. It is particularly important to note that I do *not* recommend chaplains work beyond their normal hours as a standard practice. To do that on a regular basis is not only unwise but can also reveal a tendency toward over-functioning that could be a symptom of a deeper inner struggle or pathology. Maintaining a relationship with a spiritual director or faith companion can

> *Regularly working beyond scheduled hours is unwise and can reveal a tendency toward over-functioning.*

assist in setting healthy boundaries, along with helping to unpack the emotional and spiritual effects of ministering to others.

The stories of Sara, Hunter, Jeff, Jordan, and Eli in chapters four through eight, emphasize the quality of self-care that calls on chaplains to cultivate camaraderie among staff members. Through collaborative and collegial relationships, I have been able to process the impact from an exceptionally traumatic event, feel the satisfaction of recognizing that my work truly makes a difference in someone's life, and even experience the release that laughter brings after a particularly funny experience. Someone once asked me, "Who chaplains the chaplain?" I quickly replied, "Another chaplain." Those involved in similar ministry have the best understanding of the work, feelings, and processes. Experienced chaplain colleagues are trusted voices and always available to offer a clearer perspective when our instincts become clouded.

I strive to nurture my love of being a chaplain with it countless tragedies and sorrows while not losing sight of my own humanity and needs.

Since there will always be more needs in hospital, hospice, or clinic environments than there are chaplains to meet those needs, I frequently reflect on the growing necessity for, and wisdom found in, the concept of self-care. Listed below are some of the key points about self-care and what it means to me. The chart demonstrates ways in which I nurture my love of being a chaplain with its countless tragedies and sorrows while at the same time not losing sight of my own humanity and needs. Everyone needs nurturing, chaplains included. A great joy comes over me when I nurture the memories of where I have been and how far I have come. Maya Angelou eloquently reminds us, "We delight in the beauty of the butterfly, but rarely admit the changes it has gone through to achieve that beauty." I am forever thankful for the transformational quality of this ministry—for me as well as for those who permitted me to birth their sacred stories. I am honored to be a *Spiritual Midwife!*

COMPONENTS OF SELF-CARE

S	Stipulate	Caregivers need healthy boundaries. With the help of a counselor or mentor, find a way to define and *stipulate* your personal and professional boundaries.
E	*Eliminate*	Over-functioning in your role as chaplain is lethal. Learn about and *eliminate* the ways in which you tend to over-function. Replace those tendencies with healthier options.
L	*Locate*	*Locate* a spiritual director/mentor and sustain the relationship with that faith companion to help keep you connected to your spiritual source.
F	*Facilitate*	No one understands the ministry of chaplains like other chaplains. *Facilitate* the development of collaborative relationships by sharing stresses and successes.
-		
C	*Cultivate*	Humor has marvelous medicinal value. Whenever you have an opportunity to *cultivate* laughter, please do it– you'll feel better for it.
A	*Appreciate*	Learn to recognize and *appreciate* that your efforts actually make a difference. Also, remember and *appreciate* that you are part of a team and you alone are not called upon to rescue or save anyone.
R	*Recuperate*	Spend time away from work every week doing something that *recuperates* and restores your body, mind, and spirit; such as walking, reading, writing, photography, poetry, quilting, scrap-booking, bicycling, running, painting, etc.
E	*Evaluate*	Periodically *evaluate* your reasons for becoming a chaplain, rejoice in all you have learned since CPE, celebrate the transformation you have experienced, and then write down one thing that keeps you coming back to work each day.

Wisdom Prayer:

Insightful One,

Please hear my prayer this day as I ask you to *grant me the quietude* needed *to nurture my sense of calling* when days are demanding and long; *a steadfast* and compassionate *heart* necessary *to bear the trials of others* without breaking under the emotional weight; *and* when each pastoral visit concludes and each day ends, *the understanding* that *my ministry is meaningful* in ways that are sometimes beyond my earthly comprehension.

And regardless of the situation, *in all things, may I give thanks*. Amen.

Reflective Questions:

- Recall a situation or event in your life when you felt the emotional weight of being a caregiver. What were some of the feelings you experienced?
- What is your insight or opinion about my choice to stay beyond my normal work hours with the family of the trauma victim? What would you have done? Why?
- To whom do you turn as a confidant when your body, mind, and spirit need nurturing? What are the qualities and characteristics of your "go to person" that give you a sense of trust and value in his/her ability to nurture you?
- How do you arrive at the awareness you are in need? What are the signs your spirit is feeling depleted?
- What does *self-care* mean to you? When do you allow yourself to take time out for renewing your mind and spirit? What could you do for yourself that feels restorative?
- Maya Angelou's quote reminds us of the transformational struggle of the butterfly. In what ways have you been changed by your chosen vocation?
- What would you add to or change in the Self-Care chart?

Blessed are the wise, for they understand the value of self-care.

Prayer Matters

Calling Prayer

Source of Universal Life,

Are you calling from the moment of birth, or have you implanted the seed of desire for your purpose, as I was knitted together in my mother's womb? Is the seed of my calling blossoming in frustration or nurtured by the loving waters of supportive family and friends recognizing the gift within? If you are calling me to chaplaincy, may I not hesitate, but instead respond with gentle curiosity to all the ways you seek to gain my attention and speak to my heart.

Persistent Hound of Heaven, awaken my longings to the needs and hunger of the world that I might recognize the cries of the hopeful and the hopeless, newborn and elderly, pampered and neglected, those fighting for life and the suicidal, the godly and godless. Grant me ears to hear their silent cries, hands strong enough to hold their pain, and give me a heart tender enough to care for each one as Imago Dei. Amen.

Calling Prayer "Within"

Source of Universal Life,

Seed of my calling, with gentle curiosity awaken my hopeful neglected ears to hear; and give me a heart tender enough to care for each as Imago Dei. Amen.

Preparation Prayer

Omniscient One,

I ponder daily and pray unceasingly about this service of holy trust to which you have called me. I knock, I seek, I ask, and I await the embrace of your potter's hands to mold and make of me a sacred vessel. Teach me how to witness a final breath. Guide me in the ways to hold a mother's tears. Grant me wisdom to release a soul to you.

Touch the hollows of my heart with your warm compassion, fill me to overflowing with your unconditional love, prepare me to be a reflection of your abiding spirit, and expand my often unyielding spirit. Transform me into a spacious container that I might carry back to you the tears of joy and of sorrow. May the holiness of our tears water and bring forth new life. Empty me to begin again. Amen.

Preparation Prayer "Within"

Omniscient One,

I pray unceasingly. I await your potter's hands. Teach me, guide me, grant me wisdom. Fill me, prepare me, expand my spirit. Transform me into a spacious container. Empty me to begin again. Amen.

Presence Prayer

Ever-Present One,

Gently remind us of young Samuel's loving response as you summoned him. Samuel said, "Speak, Lord, for your servant is listening." How often we demand, "Listen, Lord, for your servant is speaking." Speak to our hearts so we hear you over the incessant noise of this fast-paced world. Please slow our pace, unplug us from the addictive temptations of technology, and help us listen deeply to one another.

May we gift each other with the blessing of true presence so our weary, troubled souls might begin to heal. As we become quiet, may the world grow in stillness. As we listen, may all ears be opened. As we heal, may our world be renewed. Amen.

Presence Prayer "Within"

Ever-Present One,

Speak, Lord, for your servant is listening. Speak to our hearts. Slow our pace. Help us listen deeply to one another. May troubled souls begin to heal. May the world grow in stillness. May our world be renewed. Amen.

Compassion Prayer

God of Comfort,

The warmth of Divine consolation provides comfort when I am afflicted and permeates every step of my human journey. May I strive to embody you as I accept your invitations to weep with those who weep, to comfort those in need of comforting, and to wade into and bear witness to the pain and suffering of others without judgment.

Your children are hurting. Compassion is messy. Compassion is not easy. Compassion begs for action. I will follow. Show me the way. Amen.

Compassion Prayer "Within"

God of Comfort,

Divine consolation permeates my human journey. I accept your invitations to comfort and bear witness to suffering without judgment. Compassion is messy, not easy, begs for action. Show me the way. Amen.

Accountability Prayer

Gracious Advocate,

As the universe unfolds, opportunities abound for me to stand up and to speak out on behalf of the voiceless. Like a turtle longing for the comfort of a safe shell, I tend to hide from all that scares me. Hesitation and fear too often keep me ineffective and paralyzed. I miss the chance to reach out and help someone in need.

Living in community, I have a responsibility for the well-being of others. Grace me with courage to make a difference in big and small ways. When I am faced with decisions and I am tempted to pull back, support my efforts to move toward life-giving choices. May I risk what I think is a shelter from the storm for the firmness of my convictions. Amen.

Accountability Prayer "Within"

Gracious Advocate,

Opportunities abound to speak out. I tend to hide. Hesitation and fear keep me paralyzed.

I have a responsibility. Grace me, when I am tempted to pull back, to move toward the firmness of my convictions. Amen.

Mindfulness Prayer

Boundless Love,

Come walk with me through the fertile fields of life; and come sit awhile with me by the stream of a thousand difficult decisions. Come lift me up from the anguish of uncertainty and linger with me in the fragrant gardens of justice; and bask in the sunlit terrain of cultural sensitivity. Come hold my hand and guide my feet toward the light of each new day; and then come rest with me in the spaciousness and serenity of loving choices.

Come. Open the windows of my heart. Amen.

Mindfulness Prayer "Within"

Boundless Love,

Walk with me and sit awhile by the stream of difficult decisions. Lift me from uncertainty. Linger in the fragrant gardens and bask in cultural sensitivity. Hold my hand and rest with me in the serenity of loving choices.

Open the windows of my heart. Amen.

Collaboration Prayer

Spirit of Oneness,

May all creation sing unending rhythms of harmony into my heart when I feel connected and especially when I feel disconnected. May songs of cooperation stimulate my personal and professional goals. May melodies of collaboration rejuvenate my weary spirit. May themes of interdependence stir my imagination toward peaceful solutions.

And as I celebrate my own unique contributions, may the music of unity remind me of the healing quality of working alongside kindred spirits as co-laborers in the shared ministry of love, always for the greater good of the world. Amen.

Collaboration Prayer "Within"

Spirit of Oneness,

Sing into my heart songs of cooperation, melodies of collaboration, themes of interdependence.

And the music of unity, always for the greater good of the world. Amen.

Authenticity Prayer

Mystical Reality,

The world is not an easy place to walk as my true self. Distractions of false gods tempt me to put on masks that hide who I really am. Remind me daily that you love me as I am. You do not ask me to be an improved version of someone else. You call me to the table of authenticity, to be the person you created me to be. Breathe in me breath of God. That I may live and breathe and have my being in you, please live and breathe and have your being in me.

Shine your light of genuine love on me so that I may, in turn, radiate your goodness, the Divine DNA of authenticity, toward everyone I meet, and especially toward myself. Amen.

Authenticity Prayer "Within"

Mystical Reality,

Distractions tempt me to hide who I really am. Love me; call me to the table of authenticity. Breathe in me, that I may live.

Shine your light of genuine love, that I may radiate authenticity. Amen.

Wisdom Prayer:

Insightful One,

Please hear my prayer this day as I ask you to grant me the quietude needed to nurture my sense of calling when days are demanding and long; a steadfast and compassionate heart necessary to bear the trials of others without breaking under the emotional weight; and when each pastoral visit concludes and each day ends, the understanding that my ministry is meaningful in ways that are sometimes beyond my earthly comprehension.

And regardless of the situation, in all things, may I give thanks. Amen.

Wisdom Prayer "Within"

Insightful One,

Grant me the quietude to nurture my sense of calling, a steadfast heart to bear the trials of others, and the understanding my ministry is meaningful.

And in all things, may I give thanks. Amen.

Photography Matters

Chapter One – Be Called: Late one evening, I sat at my dining table contemplating ways to visually depict the concept of "Calling." My eyes fell on a book titled *God Calling*. This book was given to me during a transitional time in my life by my dear friend Louise and has been a wonderful source of spiritual nourishment over the years. The Old Testament passage from Isaiah came to mind simultaneously. I quickly found my camera and began shooting, changing angles and lighting with each photo. After shooting more than a dozen photos, I selected the best one of the group. It happened to be the first photo taken that evening.

Chapter Two – Be Prepared: The photograph of the tiny watering can sitting next to the gloriously healthy airplane plant was taken on the porch of a high school friend's country home on the outskirts of Tallahassee. Jacqui hosted a delightful girls' getaway weekend for four women who have known each other since seventh grade. At the time, the image of the small antique watering can prepared to nourish the growing plant seemed reminiscent of our well-tended and still flourishing friendships.

Chapter Three – Be Present: One night, several years ago, I packed up my camera and tripod and drove to the beach to capture the full *moonrise* on Pensacola Beach. I became completely enraptured with setting up the tripod and aiming my camera perfectly toward where the moon would begin to peek over the water. Once every detail was checked and rechecked, I watched and waited for the moon. The sudden noise of children behind me caused me to turn around. What I saw was a most spectacular *sunset*. The sky was ablaze with the setting sun that had gone unnoticed because I was waiting for the moon. I swung my camera around just in time to snap two photos before the sun disappeared out of sight. My lesson in being present was noted.

Chapter Four – Be Compassionate: During a lunch break from a pediatric chaplains' conference in Houston, a colleague drove us through historic Glenwood Cemetery. This particular cemetery is dotted with extraordinary monuments, many of which are angels. I was drawn to this specific angel and photographed her from various angles. Walking around her brought me to tears as I imagined her sense of loss. Although her face is unseen, her posture, head position, arms, hands, and the fluid drape of her garment speak volumes about her overwhelming sorrow and abiding compassion.

Chapter Five – Be Accountable: When I began my year-long chaplain residency program, I underwent a barrage of psychological testing. Among those tests were the Myers-Briggs and the Johari Window. Having just transitioned from twenty-plus years in technology, my score in the Johari Window testing classified me as a "Turtle." I was reluctant to reveal much about myself. Turtles tend to keep their head tucked in and hope to be left undisturbed. Upon leaving CPE, my supervisor remarked that I was "no longer a turtle." So, when I discovered these wonderful and playful turtles in a pond outside Albuquerque, I photographed them with their necks outstretched. Watching them, I realized how difficult it can be to stand up for what you believe. Doing so sometimes means we have to stick our necks out—a phrase that is symbolic for taking risks.

Chapter Six – Be Mindful: Windows and doors intrigue me. In August 2011, I attended a summer theology intensive at the University of Oxford in the UK. This was not only an unforgettable learning experience but also an unforgettable photographic exploration. With only a smartphone camera, I shot over two hundred pictures. On my last day in Oxford, I sat on the window seat in my dorm room, reflecting on the blessings of the trip and feeling melancholy about leaving. When I got up to begin packing for the trip home, I noticed the way the light was streaming through the window and snapped this photo just before walking out the door.

Chapter Seven – Be Collaborative: From the moment I decided to include a be-attitude of collaboration, I knew this photograph would be its symbolic representation. On a central Texas day trip with my husband and another couple, we came across these five colorful Adirondack chairs. Rainy weather had somewhat dampened our adventuresome spirits. But as we walked through this quaint space with its charming shops, the rain abruptly halted long enough for me to take this picture. Each chair is unique in color but matching in style. All were arranged in a way that seemed to invite a collaborative conversation.

Chapter Eight – Be Authentic: Ah, the bluebonnet! It is the state flower of Texas. When Texas winter is especially wet, the result is a spring with magnificent patches of bluebonnets along the highways and byways of the state. Artists have captured fields of bluebonnets that look as though someone spread a deep blue blanket all the way to the horizon. One morning, as I parked my car in the hospital parking lot, I noticed this lone bluebonnet growing up between the asphalt and concrete curb. It could have been any flower, but it happened to be a bluebonnet. What fascinated me was how this flower was being exactly what it was created to be, despite the harsh surroundings of concrete, asphalt, parked cars, and trampling footsteps. What better way to signify authenticity?

Chapter Nine – Be Wise: I still maintain a butterfly journal about the numerous "sightings" I have experienced since the death of my friend Judy. One of my favorite entries is when the monarch butterflies migrated right over Amarillo. I watched as they hung in clusters from a red oak tree in the neighbor's yard. Mesmerized by the beauty of hundreds of monarchs huddled together, I neglected to capture them in a photograph. Years later, at the Butterfly House in Navarre, I managed to get this close-up shot of a spectacular orange and black butterfly. Butterflies are often used to symbolize new life. Ending *The Be-Attitudes of Chaplaincy* with a photo of a butterfly in a chapter on wisdom seems a natural way to honor the remarkable gift of friendship Judy gave me in life and the continuous blessings of chaplaincy she has provided me since her death.

Reading Matters

Suggested Reading:

Capps, Donald. *Agents of Hope: A Pastoral Psychology*. Eugene: Wipf and Stock Publishers, 2001. Print.

Coles, Robert. *The Spiritual Life of Children*. Boston: Houghton Mifflin Company, 1990. Print.

Dossey, Larry, and M.D. *Healing Words: The Power of Prayer and the Practice of Medicine*. New York: HarperCollins, 1993. Print.

Fitchett, George. *Assessing Spiritual Needs: A Guide for Caregivers*. Lima: Academic Renewal Press, 2002. Print.

Fowler, James W. *Stages of Faith: The Psychology of Human Development and the Quest for Meaning*. New York: HarperOne, 1995. Print.

Grossoehme, Daniel H. *The Pastoral Care of Children*. New York: The Haworth Pastoral Press, 1999. Print.

Hart, Tobin. *The Secret Spiritual World of Children*. Makawao: Inner Ocean Publishing, Inc., 2003. Print.

Kinast, Robert L. *If Only You Recognized God's Gift: John's Gospel as an Illustration of Theological Reflection*. Grand Rapids: Wm. B. Eerdmans Publishing Co., 1993. Print.

---. *Let Ministry Teach: A Guide to Theological Reflection*. Collegeville: The Liturgical Press, 1996. Print.

Koenig, Harold G. *Spirituality in Patient Care: Why, How, When, and What*. Pennsylvania: Templeton Press, 2007. Print.

Lartey, Emmanuel Y. *Pastoral Theology in an Intercultural World.* Cleveland: The Pilgrim Press, 2006. Print.

Lester, Andrew D. *Hope in Pastoral Care and Counseling.* Louisville: Westminster John Knox Press, 1995. Print.

---. *When Children Suffer: A Sourcebook for Ministry with Children in Crisis.* Philadelphia: The Westminster Press, 1987. Print.

Miller, James E. *The Art of Being a Healing Presence: A Guide for Those in Caring Relationships.* Fort Wayne: Willowgreen Publishing, 2001. Print.

Nichols, Michael P, PhD. *The Lost Art of Listening: How Learning to Listen Can Improve Relationships.* New York: The Guilford Press, 1995. Print.

Niklas, Gerald R., Rev. *The Making of a Pastoral Person.* New York: Alba House, 1981. Print.

Nouwen, Henri J.M. *The Wounded Healer: Ministry in Contemporary Society.* New York: Doubleday, 1972. Print.

Oates, Wayne E. *Pastoral Counseling.* Philadelphia: The Westminster Press, 1974. Print.

Palmer, Parker J. *Let Your Life Speak: Listening for the Voice of Vocation.* San Francisco: Jossey-Bass, 2000. Print.

Pargament, Kenneth I. *Spiritually Integrated Psychotherapy: Understanding and Addressing the Sacred.* New York: The Guilford Press, 2007. Print.

Roberts, Stephen B., ed. *Professional Spiritual & Pastoral Care: A Practical Clergy and Chaplain's Handbook.* Woodstock: SkyLight Paths Publishing, 2011. Print.

Taylor, Elizabeth Johnston. *What Do I Say?: Talking with Patients about Spirituality.* Philadelphia: Templeton Foundation Press, 2007. Print.

Stone, Howard W., and James O. Duke. *How to Think Theologically.* Minneapolis: Fortress Press, 1996. Print.

VandeCreek, Larry, and Arthur M. Lucas. *The Discipline for Pastoral Care Giving: Foundations for Outcome Oriented Chaplaincy.* New York: The Haworth Press, Inc., 2001. Print.

Wimberly, Edward P. *Recalling Our Own Stories: Spiritual Renewal for Religious Caregivers.* San Francisco: Jossey-Bass, 1997. Print.

51465760R00118

Made in the USA
Charleston, SC
20 January 2016